T0193726

CHOSEN
BEFORE
BIRTH

The missionary biography
of Ruthie Burt Cornwell

Ruthie Burt Cornwell

WESTBOW
PRESS®
A DIVISION OF THOMAS NELSON
& ZONDERVAN

Copyright © 2019 Ruthie Burt Cornwell.

All rights reserved. No part of this book may be used or reproduced by
any means, graphic, electronic, or mechanical, including photocopying,
recording, taping or by any information storage retrieval system
without the written permission of the author except in the case of
brief quotations embodied in critical articles and reviews.

This book is a work of non-fiction. Unless otherwise noted, the author
and the publisher make no explicit guarantees as to the accuracy of
the information contained in this book and in some cases, names of
people and places have been altered to protect their privacy.

WestBow Press books may be ordered through booksellers or by contacting:

WestBow Press
A Division of Thomas Nelson & Zondervan
1663 Liberty Drive
Bloomington, IN 47403
www.westbowpress.com
1 (866) 928-1240

Because of the dynamic nature of the Internet, any web addresses or
links contained in this book may have changed since publication and
may no longer be valid. The views expressed in this work are solely those
of the author and do not necessarily reflect the views of the publisher,
and the publisher hereby disclaims any responsibility for them.

Any people depicted in stock imagery provided by Getty Images are models,
and such images are being used for illustrative purposes only.
Certain stock imagery © Getty Images.

Scripture quotations taken from the New American Standard
Bible® (NASB), Copyright © 1960, 1962, 1963, 1968, 1971, 1972,
1973, 1975, 1977, 1995 by The Lockman Foundation
Used by permission. www.Lockman.org

ISBN: 978-1-9736-6759-9 (sc)
ISBN: 978-1-9736-6758-2 (e)

Print information available on the last page.

WestBow Press rev. date: 08/13/2019

CONTENTS

FOREWORD

The story you are about to read is of a little girl from a town in Northwestern Pennsylvania who knows that she was destined to be a missionary before she was born. I first knew her as Ruthie Morrow, when she came to our home for one of her first mission assignments, to babysit me and my siblings! Several years later I got to know her as Ruth Burt, who with her husband George, told me and several other young people in our church some amazing stories of mission work in Bolivia and Peru. Finally, I have had the privilege of knowing her as Ruth Cornwell, who with her husband Bob, continues to serve the Lord as a "home missionary" to this very day.

Based on my knowledge of Ruth, I can testify that she, like Jeremiah, was "set apart" before she was born to be a missionary. As her story reveals, she has been a faithful bearer of the gospel of Jesus Christ everywhere she has lived, resulting in many, many people being "born again" of the Spirit (John 3:3-8). Actually, she also helped some of those same people be born the first time, when much to her surprise, Ruth became a medical missionary! You, too, will be surprised and amazed as you read her story.

Dr. Edward "Ed" Huntley

I have been privileged to know and consider Ruthie Cornwell as a friend for nearly 30 years. It was my honor to perform the wedding ceremony for her and Bob Cornwell nearly 25 years ago. In addition, I worked alongside them in the construction of two churches in northern Peru located in the villages of Tushmo and San Lorenzo.

Ruthie has had an incredible life ministry, both in South America and the United States. She has been blessed to see many saved as a missionary and healed by the medical practices she has performed as a nurse. She and Bob are loved and are a blessing to all who have been given the opportunity to know them. This was evidenced to me on one trip to Tushmo, Peru, in which I witnessed hundreds who walked for hours to welcome her back to the village.

I think you will be deeply blessed as well as you read this book of her life. It details the many opportunities God has given her to serve as a missionary and nurse. I think you will agree that she will have a great reward in heaven for her faithfulness.

Dr. Byron A. "Butch" Lee, ThD, DD, MA

PREFACE AND ACKNOWLEDGEMENTS

Glory be to the Lord. I would like to acknowledge my Lord and Savior Jesus Christ for His blessed call upon my life. That He chose such as I to be His full-time servant for more than fifty-seven years brings great humbleness to my soul. I still want to do what I can for Him in my aged years. Such a blessing He provided me by allowing me to follow in His footsteps. He and only He deserves praise and honor.

Recognition must be given to George, my wonderful enabler and caring partner in all my efforts to serve God. I thank God for permitting such a godly man to walk by my side through so many years. To the others through the years who gave encouragement and support when much needed, thank you. For all who offered up prayers on George's and my behalf, I will be always grateful. "But the Spirit Himself intercedes for us with groanings too deep for words; and He who searches the hearts knows what the mind of the Spirit is, because He intercedes for the saints according to the will of God" Romans 8:26-27.

Several individuals of my church, McCalla Bible Church, were used by God to encourage the writing of *Chosen Before Birth*. May God's approval for each individual's contribution be a blessing to each soul. To Tom and Glenda Massengale, Becky

Ernest, Clara Jordan, Patsy Smith, Ann Brown, Melissa Smith, Whitney Napier, all who provided assistance in getting the story written, I wish to give a heartfelt thank you.

As I have retold some of my life stories, I am sure that I may have unintentionally recalled things out of order or remembered some details through the fog of many years, but I have done my best to paint a true picture of our experiences as missionaries. Some names have been changed as it is not my intention to bring judgment or shame on anyone mentioned. I hope these experiences will inspire others who may be led to serve the Lord as we were.

Ruth "Ruthie" Burt Cornwell

CHAPTER ONE

CHOSEN

"Before I formed you in the womb I knew you,
and before you were born I consecrated you;
I have appointed you a prophet to the nations."
Jeremiah 1:5

Harry John and Bessie Louise Morrow lived with their four children on a small 48-acre farm in northwestern Pennsylvania. The farm was located on Route 5, five miles from the town of Cochranton. On this farm, there was a long lane which ran downhill between two large fields of corn, wheat and potatoes. The lane led lazily down in the direction of an old, somewhat-green house. Due to the passage of time- and hard times at that- it was in desperate need of repair, especially repainting. This the Morrows called home for many years.

Harry Morrow worked as a blacksmith for the WPA- the Works Progress Administration, part of Roosevelt's New Deal which provided jobs building highways, streets, bridges, parks and other projects. He earned very little income, but he did his very best to subsidize his meager earnings to provide for his growing family. One way he kept the family going was to plant a large garden with plenty of potatoes and vegetables. God blessed his efforts and the Morrow family knew no hunger as others often did during this time.

Harry and Bessie had three boys, Carl, Ed and John, and one girl, Martha. And now they were expecting their fifth child. In Pennsylvania, although the calendar said it was spring, patches of snow and ice remained. Such were the conditions when a tragedy (as some would call it) occurred only three weeks before I was born. The steps at the front of the house were icy and Mom slipped, resulting in a nasty fall and an injured spine. She wondered if the fall had endangered the baby she carried. She was consoled by the fact that she could feel the baby kicking and moving. When I, Ruth Louise Morrow, was born on April 21, 1934, a blood clot covered my entire head. I still bear a large scar as the evidence of our icy ordeal but greater still, of God's mercy. Years later, Mom told me that even before my birth, she believed that I had been chosen for something special. She said, "God has something for you."

I recall a time when I was about four years old that Martha and I were playing on the porches at our house. The house had two porches: one for the living room entrance, the other for the entrance to the kitchen. A wooden plank had been placed over the gap between the two porches to enable passage from one to the other. One summer day, we kids were having a ball, running back and forth between the porches. As usually happens with children, we tired of just going back and forth and sought new excitement. I took an interest in the rain barrel that resided in the gap, between the wooden plank and the house. Moving excitedly to the water-filled barrel, I peered in and saw a little girl looking back at me. Wide-eyed and amazed to find a playmate right there in our rain barrel, I leaned still farther. Suddenly, I lost my balance and fell in headfirst. Gasping for air and frightened, I was ever so glad when I felt two strong, firm hands pulling me upward and out of the barrel. I don't think I need to say that I was then given to understand that never, never were we kids to play around that barrel. I was sad to lose my new playmate so quickly, but I was very glad to be out of that barrel!

Those porches often proved to be a training ground as well as a gathering place. One summer afternoon, some of us were gathered on the porch. It was hot and there were no air conditioners. Dad was giving Ed and John a "baldy haircut." This was a cut which looked just like it sounds, and it would make my brothers much cooler in the summer heat. As the boys were getting their haircuts, Martha and I were playing with our little iron. It was a real iron, used for ironing clothing, and it was very heavy. For some reason forgotten now, Martha got mad and threw the iron at me. While the boys got haircuts, I got a good size cut just above my right eye. Thankfully, Mom had the skill to care for my eye amidst all the commotion, and Dad had the skill to complete the boys' haircuts. But this outdoor episode revealed that Dad's true skill was in delivering a lesson concerning temper. After he had cooled the boys down, he warmed up Martha's bottom quite well, proving that Dad could qualify as both a heating and an air-conditioning man!

The outdoors offered even more fun for us light-hearted, adventurous kids. We especially enjoyed the barn, playing in the haymow, jumping from the high part to the lower area. There was also a straw mow on the other side of the barn, next to the outside wall. We had great fun crawling through the tunnels we made there. There was a large black walnut tree in the middle of the front yard, and there, Dad had put a swing on a large branch. Many happy hours were spent there, dreaming of wonderful things.

All three of my brothers were very good at making box kites. Every summer, each made his own kite. Give them some paper, cross-sticks, glue, string, a rag to make a tail, and, in a short time, the three of them would have air creations fit for many hours of running to catch air currents for their kites to ride in the warm sun.

Always ready to use their imaginations on lazy summer days, Ed and John decided they wanted a swimming pool. Since there was no Walmart back then, the boys went to work, lugging rocks and sticks and mud to dam up the creek that ran through the pasture. After a lot of time, sweat and hard work, they had themselves a nice swimming hole. We kids often caught minnows at the creek, almost instantly letting them go. It was just the challenge of the catch that we enjoyed. We also liked to catch the crabs that scurried away to hide from us by burrowing deep in the sand. This was our special place for laughter and fun, and I like to think of it as God's playground created just for us.

We knew how to entertain ourselves, but we also knew the result of disobedience and poor judgment, and we had a healthy respect for authority. We learned not to talk back to our parents, not to be sassy, nor to even complain much. If we did, we knew that punishment would be the outcome. Sometimes green willow switches were used on the bare legs, and, oh, how it would sting! My dad had a razor strap on which he sharpened his straight-edge razor, and it was sometimes used in a way not one of us wanted to face. What a lasting lesson that strap carried with every stroke. Even though we had never heard the words of Colossians 3:20, "Children, be obedient to your parents in all things, for this is well-pleasing to the Lord," we learned to obey!

I learned the strap lesson when my curiosity about the family clock got the best of me. I knew that the clock was hands-off, but overcome by temptation, I turned the hands and changed the time. That may not sound so bad, but having only one clock, it was important for it to be accurate. As Dad laid the strap on my backside, I learned a lesson in obedience, a respect for authority, and the reason the others didn't want to face that strap. I never wanted to meet with the strap again, and I never did!

Dad, about six feet tall and quiet with red hair, said what he meant and was known for always keeping his word. Everyone who knew him knew that he was an honest man. How proud we kids were to call him our Dad!

Mom was short- only four feet and eleven inches tall- with beautiful, long, dark hair which she wore in a bun at the back of her head, and she made a lovely picture for all of us. We always chose to be near her, playing at her feet when we were small. Like my dad, she meant what she said, and she knew just how to keep a house full of kids well in hand. How grateful I am for my parents and the character they instilled in me!

Mom and Dad created many pleasurable times, giving us special memories during a time which afforded few luxuries. Dad often got down on hands and knees to give us the best piggyback rides ever had by anyone. Mom often read stories to us as we sat around her in the old rocking chair. Our parents were very loving, though there was not much hugging and kissing. Theirs was true parental love, the kind of love that acts in behalf of others, the kind that taught us to be truthful and to live by good standards, such as the "Golden Rule." We didn't yet know that Matthew 7:12 said, "Treat people the same way you want them to treat you," but we learned to do that from our parents.

Winter brought extra challenges for Dad. If his car radiator froze during a cold Pennsylvania night, he would not be able to go to work. To prevent this, Dad would sweep the barn floor clean, careful to avoid risk of fire, and park his car there with a lighted kerosene lantern on the floor beneath the radiator. Sometimes snow drifts accumulated in the driveway. Then Dad would bring the horses out of the barn and hitch them to a doubletree, a pivoted swinging bar to which the traces of a harness are fastened and by which a vehicle can be drawn. This extra work enabled Dad to fulfill his obligation to his employer and to provide for his family.

The combination of an uninsulated house and sub-zero temperatures made it necessary for the stove to be kept burning twenty-four hours a day. Wood had to be cut and chopped for the black pot-bellied stove in the living room and for the wood-burning stove in the kitchen. I remember watching Dad and my brothers cut logs with the crosscut saw, a saw designed chiefly to cut across the grain of wood. After cutting the logs into smaller sections, they would then split those sections with an ax, preparing even smaller pieces for the stoves. This work continued during the long, cold winter months.

We girls were not left out of the work scene. Mother took care of the cooking and housecleaning and most of the indoor tasks, while Martha and I set the table and washed the dishes. Mom's work also included making sure we left for school on time. On very cold days, Mom would go to the barn and prepare the horse to transport us to school. With no school bus to depend on, this spared us from walking almost a mile to school in the extreme cold.

Our school was quite different from the schools of today. It was a one-room school with the same teacher for all eight grades. The teacher moved around the room, going from one grade to the next, helping the children with the same subject but at different levels. While the teacher was with others, the rest of the class would do homework.

Carl, our oldest brother, had severe asthma, and at the age of fourteen, it was determined that he would need to leave the farm to get away from the dust, hay and straw. He moved to a small town where he was able to work in a factory sweeping floors and doing other odd jobs.

Our life was simple but full of activity. Spring brought the time for planting a garden. Summer brought chores of watering and weeding. Mom taught us from a young age how to recognize the difference between the weeds and the good plants. At harvest time, there were the jobs of shelling peas and husking corn. Mom canned as many things as she could, and she also preserved the corn by use of a corn dryer. A corn dryer was a large rectangular pan, long enough to cover two burners on the stove. There were two parts: the open top part where the fresh corn was placed and the lower part which was filled with water. As the water boiled, the moisture in the corn evaporated, leaving it dry and hard. Now it was ready to be put in bags to be stored for winter. When we were ready to eat it, Mom soaked the corn in water overnight to bring it to a soft state, ready to cook. Potatoes, cabbage and carrots were put in the cellar to be brought out as needed. Some times were more difficult than others, and I remember a time when Mom said she was lacking four main staples: flour, cornmeal, sugar and salt.

Dad often went hunting so our family had an occasional rabbit to eat with Mom's delicious dumplings, pinches of biscuit dough dropped into soup and allowed to boil. Every year in late fall, Dad butchered a cow or a pig. After cutting the meat in large pieces, he packed the pieces into big wooden barrels filled with salt to keep the meat from spoiling. Then, on days when cold, icy winds blew, we were warmed by a hot, well-prepared meal due to the mutual efforts of a hard-working family.

One of the most difficult but necessary chores was the wash. My first memory of helping with the wash was when I was four years old. Martha and I helped Mom by taking turns using the clothes stomper in a large galvanized tub filled with hot water and Fells Naphtha soap. The stomper had two layers of metal attached to a wooden handle, and each of these layers had small holes along the sides with about a quarter-inch space between. As we moved the stomper up and down, our arms grew tired, but the clothes were cleaned.

We had an old, very large, iron wood-burning stove in the kitchen. Here Mom put clothes in a copper, oval-shaped boiler filled with soap and water. Wash day was especially hard because we had to go down a hill to get the water and then carry the water back up the hill to the house. Martha and I helped Mom wring out the clothes, each taking an end of an item, twisting it in opposite directions. Together we were able to wring even large items. We always hung the clothes on a clothesline strung between the house, the milk house and the corn crib. The clothes blew in the wind, soaking up the warm sunshine. We all loved the fresh smell of clothes hung outside to dry.

Later, Dad and Mom were able to purchase a used Maytag washer with a gas motor. Because of the fumes and the noise of the motor, the washer had to be placed so that the exhaust hose could run out of a window. That washer made wash day so much easier, even though it didn't seem to like me very much. One time my hair got caught in the wringer, and, on another occasion, a fingernail was pulled off. Such sacrifices were small, all things considered. This was so much better than washing and wringing by hand.

With no electricity, the ironing was done with flatirons heated on the kitchen stove. As the iron in use began to cool, we switched to one still heating on the stove. The irons came in various weights. The heavier the iron, the better the clothes would be pressed. There were no drip-dry clothes in those days, so all outer clothes and sometimes even "unmentionables" had to be ironed. Boy, did I hate ironing! Would you believe, some people even ironed their pillowcases and sheets!

Another chore that could be an issue was the "slop jar." Our house had no indoor bathroom, so our bedrooms had what we called a "slop jar" or a "thundermug" which had to be emptied every day. We called it a thundermug because with no rug or carpeting, you could hear every time it was used. Every morning, someone had the dreaded task of carrying it from the house, down the hill to the outhouse. I must have been about seven years old when, on a beautiful, sunny summer day, it was my turn to empty the thundermug. As Mom pinned clothes on the clothesline, I slowly walked down the path. I remember turning to talk with Mom as I walked backwards. Well, you know what happened. I stubbed my toe and down I went, spilling the contents all over me. Mom gave me a bath and I smelled better in a short time, but laughter continued long afterwards around our house, every time the story of my mishap was retold.

When I was nine years old, Dad and Mom bought the "Fisher Memorial Works," a business previously owned by Mom's parents in the small town of East Springfield, Pennsylvania, near Lake Erie. Instructions had been given for the business to be sold to one of their children, the one who made the highest bid. My parents were the high bidders, and I was especially glad when I saw that it was located right next to the only church in town, an added gift from God.

Before my grandparents lived there, the house had been used to lodge travelers going through the area by horse and buggy. The old iron hitching posts, still in front of the house when our family moved in, remained there for years before they were eventually stolen. The interesting old house had fourteen rooms with a couple of additions, the older part of the house having been secured with wooden pegs. There were five outside doors and two stairways- plenty of space for us kids to play hide-and-seek and to have treasure hunts. We discovered a secret room not long after we moved in, and we learned that the house had once been a slave runner's house, used for hiding slaves during the Civil War. We also found a large cannonball in the house, and it must have weighed at least five pounds. It weighed enough that one would not want to drop it on one's toes, as I once did, because a five-pound cannonball can burst toes open. But don't worry; my toe healed with no problems.

We felt as if we were now uptown. We even had electricity instead of kerosene lamps. And, because of the family business, Dad and Mom had a phone. It was a party-line phone which meant that other families (parties) had phones connected to the same line. Mounted to the wall, there was a large rectangular wooden box with a crank on the right side. To make a call, one turned the crank just a little for a short ring, or longer for a long ring. We listened carefully when the phone rang to make sure the call was for family and not for someone else. Courtesy was important, and we children were taught never to listen in on other people's calls nor to stay on the line too long in case someone else needed to make a call.

Since there was no central heating, it was necessary to have a pot-bellied stove in the living room to be used during the cold winter months. As before, we had no inside bathroom. To reach the outhouse, we walked through the house, then through the woodshed and then out into the backyard where our destination was not too far away. Even though our "new" home afforded our family many new conveniences, we still had to deal with many of the same old problems.

When I was eleven and in the fifth grade, I was given a New Testament by Gideons who came to our school. The Gideons International is an association of Christian business and professional men and their wives dedicated to telling people about Jesus through providing Bibles and New Testaments. I remember seeing the small Bibles nicely stacked in neat rows on a little table. As each of us neared the table, a small New Testament was placed in our outstretched hands. I was so pleased to receive such a gift. I felt I had been given a treasure, although I did not know yet just what a rich treasure I had received. I kept my little Bible and cherished it, reading it faithfully every night.

One night, it was impressed upon my heart to bow my head and ask Jesus to be my Savior. I was thirteen years old.

I had a hunger for God's Word that seemed to create an endless desire in me to be fed. It was exciting to be with other Christians, so every time the church doors were opened, I was there. It was convenient to live next door to the church. I went to Sunday School and church services and youth group meetings. There were often missionary speakers and I was always blessed by their messages.

Also at the age of thirteen, I informed my parents that they no longer had to spend any of their money for my clothes or personal items. I intended to work to provide for myself. Before I entered high school, I had begun doing jobs to earn money to take care of my own needs.

When I was sixteen, Dad hired a man to paint our house. Dad continued to work at the business while the man painted, leaving him little time to supervise the work. As a result, the painter spent most of his time sitting instead of painting. I felt that I could do the job more efficiently, so I decided to negotiate a better deal for Dad. Dad must give the man his walking papers and I would then assume the painting of the house at a better fee. Dad accepted my bold proposal and offered me a lower price than he had been paying the non-working painter. This allowed me to give our old house a new look, earn a salary, and have the extra reward of saving my parents money.

While in high school, I cleaned houses for people, washing woodwork and scrubbing walls and floors. I even picked up potatoes when they were ready to be harvested. Once my older brother Ed and I had a contest to see who could pick up potatoes fastest. In one day, Ed gathered one hundred crates of potatoes-fast picking for a young boy. But there I was, a young girl, and I had picked up ninety-nine crates. I was so proud of myself for doing nearly as much as my big brother. Throughout summer and early fall, I picked strawberries, cherries, berries of all sorts, corn, peas, beans, tomatoes, and anything else that needed harvesting. No work was too low for me to do. I would try any task set before me.

I also took in a variety of sewing jobs. By the age of fifteen, I was taking on difficult projects for even the best of seamstresses. One such challenge was making gowns for a wedding. The future bride gave me only a picture cut from a magazine- no patterns. She simply asked if I could make those lovely gowns in the picture for her wedding. After examining the picture, I knew that I had the knowledge and the skill to complete the task. I began by determining how much fabric and other accessories would be required for each dress. I then cut the fabric and began putting the dresses together. I went to school during the day and sewed every afternoon. It took me only a couple of weeks to complete the bride's dress, two bridesmaids' dresses and a flower girl's dress. I was proud of my work which resulted in beautiful dresses that looked professionally sewn. More importantly, though, they pleased the bride. I found that I really enjoyed sewing, and through the years, I have continued to make many of my own clothes as well as items for my children.

By the time I was sixteen years old, there was no doubt that the Lord was calling me to be a missionary. I talked constantly about my call to missions; it was in my mind all day. I even dreamed about being with a group of South American natives and sharing with them the plan of salvation. I envisioned myself going to a lady's house in a clearing. There I sat on a log, surrounded by lush green trees, visiting and getting acquainted. The lady and I talked about the Lord and how He died to forgive the sins of men. This picture stayed in my mind continually. One Sunday, Pastor Augustine preached on missions. He said that his heart's desire was for someone from our church to go out as a missionary. Not long after the service, I told my pastor that

I was going to be that missionary, the first link from my church in a glorious chain of service to God.

While in high school, an assignment was given by one of our teachers, a man of Russian descent. We were instructed to write a report about our future plans, including the occupation, wages, job description, benefits and any qualifications of interest. After comparing my report with some of my classmates' reports, I discovered that my report was as well-written as others that had received a grade of B or C, but I had received a D as my grade. Had the teacher judged my report or my career choice? I knew I had written a good report about serving as a missionary but had failed to meet the teacher's expectations. From this experience I learned a lasting lesson about trusting God with disappointments.

Two years had gone by and now graduation was near. I would soon need to decide where to continue my preparation for work as a missionary. I had said in the past that I had done enough studying and had no intention of studying anymore. God often leads us to do exactly what we believed we would never do, and I soon learned not to say I would or wouldn't do certain things. More study was definitely ahead for me.

CHAPTER TWO

PREPARED

"…useful to the Master, prepared for every good work."
2 Timothy 2:21

Before graduating from high school, I had applied for a summer job at The Model Works Toy Factory. I was accepted and hired to do an assembly-line job, packing small brightly colored train sets into boxes to be sold at Christmas. Some people might consider work on an assembly line boring, but I enjoyed the job very much.

After much time in prayer that summer, I felt God leading me to Bryan University for my college education. During the famous Scopes "Monkey" Trial in 1925, William Jennings Bryan had expressed his desire for a school to be established in Dayton, Tennessee, to teach truth from a Biblical perspective. After his death later that same year, a national memorial association was formed to establish such an institution in his honor. William Jennings Bryan University opened in 1930 and, many years later in 1993, the name was shortened to Bryan College. I sent my application to Bryan University with much prayer, excitement, and a desire to get started right away.

After a few weeks, an acceptance letter from the college

arrived, bringing with it an array of emotions. This was a major undertaking on my part. I had never been such a long way away from home and family, but I trusted that God would be near to protect and guide me.

Dad did not believe it when I told him that I had been accepted to a college. As far as I knew, no one in our family or in the families of any of our relatives had ever attended any school beyond high school. I handed Dad the acceptance letter and said, "Here, Dad, read this."

He read the acceptance letter with quiet interest. "Now do you believe it?" I asked.

Slowly and reluctantly, he answered, "I guess so." But there certainly was no indication that Dad was pleased about that news. Mom, by contrast, was thrilled. She had previously told me that she was pleased that I had felt the Lord's call to missions. In their own different ways, both of my parents were supportive of my next step in that direction.

While working at the toy factory, I began to prepare suitable clothing for college. My wardrobe was quite limited. I bought two dresses to add to the few skirts and blouses I already had. This seemed to me to be enough and I felt blessed. My shoes were worn out, so a pair of shoes had to be purchased.

Now I was ready- except for the problem of transporting my bundle of belongings. It did not take long for me to realize that a suitcase was needed, a big expenditure with my limited funds. But the Lord was aware of this need and He provided in a most unexpected manner. A friend who had no way of knowing that I did not have a suitcase, mentioned one day that he had a new suitcase he wanted me to have if I needed it. Startled, my reply to this generous offer was, "Oh, yes. Thank you very much. Do you want me to go right now to your house and pick it up?" As if he understood my young enthusiastic reaction, his gracious response was to bring the suitcase to my home himself. How I appreciated his kind generosity! I was quickly discovering that our Lord has a way of knowing our needs and supplying them for us as we trust Him. "And my God will supply all your needs according to His riches in glory in Christ Jesus" (Philippians 4:19).

Now my suitcase was packed, but I still did not know how I was going to get to Bryan. After buying a few items I would need at school, I had only enough money for purchasing books, leaving no extra funds for travel. I chose not to worry about that for I had so much to rejoice about. I had my new suitcase packed and sitting by the door; I was ready to go!

On Sunday before the big day, that Tuesday known as Registration Day, I came home from a lovely service at church and sat down at the table with my family to eat dinner, treasuring these last moments together. We were talking about my leaving for the university when Dad asked again, "How are you going to get there?" The whole family's attention was now focused on me for an answer since I was planning to make a six-hundred-mile trip from East Springfield, Pennsylvania, to Dayton, Tennessee, with no travel money. I responded to Dad's question with, "I don't know, but I know I'm going."

At that moment, there was a knock at the front door. I answered the door where I found a woman I did not know. She said, "Hello," and then quietly proceeded to tell me that they had come to take me to Bryan University. I did not recognize her, and I did not know who she meant by *they*, but my heart gave a leap. Again, I was being allowed to see my God supplying all my needs, and my faith in Him was strengthened still more. It was also a thrill to see the wonderful demonstration of God's faithfulness that was being shown to my family as well.

As the lady at the door continued to talk and I continued to wonder who she was, I heard her say, "We are on our way right now and we have room in our car for you. Do you have your things ready?"

"Yes, I surely do," I answered quickly. I then excused myself to hurriedly say goodbye to my very surprised family. My suitcase was loaded into the car trunk, and as I got into the car, I realized who the lady was. In the backseat of the car sat Joanne, a friend from church who was also going to Bryan. I had seen Joanne's mother only once in passing and so did not recognize her as she stood at my door. Now I was truly on my way to Bryan!

Before we had traveled very far, I felt the need to explain that I had no money to help with the travel expenses. Joanne's mother's response to me was, "The Lord has taken care of that, so don't you be concerned." My heart sang with praise as I saw God's provision for me as His child. Jeremiah 33:3 has been my favorite scripture verse since I was saved at the age of thirteen: "Call to Me and I will answer you, and I will tell you great and mighty things, which you do not know." I did not know how I was going to get to Bryan, but my Lord knew! What a wonderful answer to my prayers!

After many hours of travel and two nights spent in motels along the way, Joanne and I arrived at Bryan University on Tuesday for Registration Day. I was assigned to a dorm room with three other girls: Jennifer from Iowa, Nancy from Chicago, and Rose from Michigan.

We four girls enjoyed dorm life and had good times together, but most of our time was spent studying. One unexpected thing that happened was that I came in one day to find my clothing drawer emptied out onto my bed. I simply put the things back into my drawer, saying nothing. Every time I left the dorm room that day, Rose emptied the drawer on my bed. Each time I put the clothing back into the drawer, I purposely chose to say nothing. I never understood why Rose would do such a thing, but the dumping took place at least five times that day. I gave no retaliation and she soon stopped.

As college life went on, I began to feel that I was not getting the courses I needed to prepare me for missionary work. I liked some of my classes, especially Old Testament Survey, taught by Alma Rader, a close relative of evangelist Paul Rader. I did not like my English class. I desired so much to take more courses that would better prepare me for the work I would actually be doing when I arrived on the mission field. After praying for God's guidance for a week, I registered for the second term as a special student, allowing me to take Christian Education courses which proved to be very helpful in my ministry to others.

Life in the dorm continued as usual, mundane and even boring. Over time, Jennifer, Nancy and I became aware that Rose was afraid of mice. We also noticed that Rose often failed to heed the curfew for being in the dorm at night. One of those nights when Rose was out late, I saw a mouse go into the broom closet and I managed to kill it. I decided to perk things up a bit. Jennifer and Nancy went along with my idea- which I now realize was a mean one. I guess I didn't believe that Rose was really as afraid of mice as she said, or maybe I just wanted to have some fun at her expense. Mean or not, I carefully put the mouse under the fold of Rose's bedspread where it tucked under the pillow.

Now Rose had the habit of unceremoniously plopping down on her bed when she came in at night. On this night, after a good bit of giggling, Jennifer, Nancy, and I settled down to wait up for Rose so that we could see her reaction. When Rose finally came in and made her usual plop on the bed, the bedspread pulled out from under the pillow and the mouse was thrown into the air. Up the mouse flew as if with wings which were guiding it straight into Rose's waiting lap. She let out a scream and then another until she was screaming continuously, grabbing at the walls. Jennifer, Nancy and I began to question the wisdom of our prank. Rose was now sweating heavily, her sobs filling the room. The resident assistant eventually heard the commotion and came in and arranged for the hysterical Rose to sleep in a different room. Eventually, Rose calmed down and seemed to forgive us for our mischief. Things returned to normal, except that I was in fear that I might be reprimanded. To my surprise, I was never called into the office to discuss the incident. I was relieved, but I also felt sorry for Rose. I was to blame for the disruption and for the pain and fear I had brought to my roommate.

During the second semester, I became very interested in a mission that worked mainly with ethnic groups in South America, called Tribes at that time. There was no doubt in my mind; I was sure that tribal work was my calling. As I prayed, I always pictured myself among tribal people. I began to pray fervently about joining this mission.

After my first year at Bryan University, I applied to New Tribes Mission, now called Ethnos360. Certain that I was following God's leadership, I continued my studies with New Tribes Mission for the next three years. Here the studies were organized somewhat differently, concentrating on the practical aspects of missions. Students studied various books of the Bible as well as news from the countries where missionaries were working. My studies there covered many aspects of missionary life, including language study and the customs and beliefs of various people groups. Especially beneficial were the lessons about friendship and the social aspects of different groups. These lessons taught the students what to do and what not to do to avoid offending the native people.

Part of the New Tribes Mission experience was a summer jungle camp. It was hands-on, learn-as-you-go work. The girls helped build their abode in the woods and then lived there for a couple of months while continuing with their other classes. The part of this experience I valued most was that chapel was held in the woods among all the wonder, colors and smells of the lush plant life. The chirping of the birds in the trees and the noises of the bugs in the bushes reminded me that even nature praises our Lord as its Creator. It was wonderful to sit in prayer for the missionaries throughout the world, seeking the Creator to meet all their needs even as we were surrounded by God's obvious provision for His beautiful creation.

The girls and boys had their own unique adventures in their camps. One day, a skunk wandered into the boys' camp and one of the boys decided to shoot it. I'm not sure the skunk was killed, but there were quite a few boys who wished they were dead themselves. The camp stank terribly for several hours. The girls were spared the worst of this episode since their home in the woods was a good distance from the boys' area.

We were a small village of people who knew little about how to live off the land. Each family of boys and girls had to do their own cooking. This led to some fun learning experiences. One night in the girls' camp, someone had forgotten to put the lid back on the jar of apple butter. Big lessons often come from small mistakes, and so it was for the girl who craved a little snack later that night. In the dark, she dug a spoon deep into the apple butter. What a shock she experienced when along with the sweetness, she encountered some unpleasantness! How she shouted as she was stung by the bees who weren't willing to share their recently discovered treat. We all decided never to eat apple butter in the dark and also always to make sure to put lids on everything after usage.

One night each week, the students were divided into groups and were assigned visitation in the nearby small towns. We usually went in pairs, witnessing to people. For our tender hearts, it was sad to realize that most of the people we met had no time or interest to hear about the Lord's love for them or to hear how He died on the cross to save them from the punishment of hell. Throughout the summer, we prayed for God to enlighten the individuals we visited. Many heard the gospel and often there were reports of people receiving Christ as their Savior.

Once we visited a pleasant Italian family. They had been fishing and were cleaning their catch. They loved to talk, and we enjoyed a wonderful time of sharing with them. As we prepared to leave, one member of the family asked if we would like some fish to take home with us. "Of course," we answered, "Yes. That would be great." After thanking them for the fish, we left, anticipating sharing our fish with others in camp and thinking about Christ feeding the multitudes.

Word came to the training camp that there was an Englishman coming to take courses in preparation for the mission field. I was asked by the director to show him around and acquaint him with the mission and the training program. I felt honored to represent the mission and I determined to reflect the Lord to this newcomer.

Mr. George Burt was a London Cockney. As George explained, "A Cockney is a person born within the sound of Bow-Bells which is within one square mile in the very heart of London. If you are not born within that particular mile, you are not a true London Cockney." He was a true London Cockney having been born within earshot of the bells of a historic church in London, St. Mary-le-Bow, and we all enjoyed his interesting dialect. I gave George a tour of the grounds, explaining the various routines and functions as we walked. George was intrigued by the jungle camp and soon joined it, moving into the boys' dorm in the woods.

As we got to know each other, I learned that George had been born in 1914 and had previously worked as an assistant to a gentleman in the House of Parliament. He had never earned a college degree but had entered the army at 26 years of age during World War II and had served for six years. As George shared with all of us in camp, I learned that his first three years included regular army duties, and he was a personal attendant to an officer. He was one of the first soldiers to volunteer as a paratrooper when the Paratrooper's Regiment began. After a time of special training and practice drops, the regiment was later sent to North Africa. The Americans were expected to come in just after the British arrived but were delayed. In an effort to provide cover for the men, the entire regiment of eighty men were dropped in a grape vineyard. Only George and one other soldier survived the vineyard and this at a cost of a great deal of shrapnel in their backs. As the two survivors struggled to get to other British personnel, they were spotted and taken prisoner by the enemy.

George and other captives were held in Italy for several months before being transferred to Germany where their treatment became worse than before. This prison camp was known as the worst camp in Germany and was infested by thousands of fleas. Flea bites were painful and often became infected. The cruelty and devaluing of life was to become a personal horror for George. Guards often pushed bayonets through soldiers' arms whether for personal entertainment, a show of authority, or because they were ordered to do so, no one knew.

Hunger was rampant and many soldiers starved to death. An elephant had died in a city zoo not far away; the prisoners were given a small piece of meat about an inch square in their soup. It was not unusual to wake up and find that a fellow soldier had died during the night. On one occasion, a soldier was so hungry that he heated his shoe polish and drank it, only to be found dead in the morning. George became very weak and thin and at one point was in a coma for two weeks. During this time, his fellow soldiers took care of him, helping him to survive.

According to the International Red Cross, there was to be no bombing near a prisoner of war camp, but the enemy did not heed this agreement. One day as George and a fellow soldier went for a walk, bombs began to drop all around them. After surviving that bomb drop, George came to the realization that God had spared his life for a reason.

The soldiers longed for change in their circumstances. In their captivity, they managed to collect some small parts from which they made a radio. In order to keep it hidden, they dissembled it and hid the parts in different places after every use of the radio. Having a link to the world outside the horrors of camp was worth the risk of such hiding. One glorious day, they heard on their radio that the war would soon be ending. True change was on the way!

When the war ended, the soldiers realized that the German guards had left the camp. George helped other soldiers to raid the food pantry before leaving to find their fellow Brits. After finding the other British soldiers, they were taken in an open-bed truck to a camp for repatriation. His three years as a prisoner had finally come to an end.

As several of us talked one evening in camp, George told us about his return home at the end of the war. He had been looking forward to a wonderful reunion with his family, but when he was discharged, he was given an address he did not recognize. Arriving at the strange address, he was greeted by one of his sisters. He learned that their home had been bombed, resulting in injury to a sister, the blindness of his father, and the death of his mother. A younger brother had also been killed while in the army in North Africa. The happy homecoming he had anticipated had become a devastating disappointment. In that moment, anger and hatred rose in his heart, but he recognized that he must not allow such negative emotions to remain. Instead, he chose not to dwell on the pain, attempting to forgive and move forward with his life.

George now began visiting churches all over London, seeking for something he felt was missing in his life. During this time, he met a London police officer, Mr. Goode, who witnessed to him and led him to receive Christ as His Savior. Mr. Goode worked with the Lattimer Youth Movement, a ministry to young boys. His influence and God's leading soon led George to surrender his life to missions. After much prayer, he was led to come to the United States to join New Tribes Mission for missionary training.

As I observed George during his time in our jungle camp, I saw that he loved children. With his jolly personality, children were drawn to him as well. I saw this as an asset which God could use to open doors for witness. It reminded me of our Lord's commandment in Mark 10:13-16: "Permit the children to come to Me; do not hinder them; for the kingdom of God belongs to such as these."

It was time for our special jungle camp to end. The single students moved back into their dorms and the couples into their individual cabins. One of the girls in my dorm had taken an interest in George. Of course, I was also interested but I had not let that be known to anyone else.

During the winter, news of an accident reached our dorm. George and several other men had gone deer hunting. As they traveled, their car hit an icy patch in the road and skidded. The door by which George was sitting was flung open, and he had been thrown from the car. How seriously he had been hurt we did not know. When I heard this news, I welled up with tears and began to pray fervently that his injury would not be very serious. It wasn't serious- only a broken leg which healed well with proper care- but I now knew just how much this man, George, meant to me.

George would often pop in to visit as I was caring for Mom Holsinger, a New Tribes Mission staff member who was ill. During these visits, I noticed that the elbows of one of his sweaters were wearing thin. When he asked if I could mend the sweater for him, I agreed. One evening as I worked at my mending, Mom recognized the sweater. With a smile on her face, she watched quietly and then said, "Knittin' for Britain, huh?" Embarrassed, I answered, "Uh, huh." I knew she realized that I cared for George. She told the director, but it was never told to any of the students and for that I was glad.

After a while, some of us students were ready to move on to language studies. George was to begin his language studies a term later. After finding this out, I felt led to spend one term with my family in Pennsylvania. When the time came to return to Wisconsin for language school, George and I started language studies the same term.

George surprised me one day following classes when he said, "I need to talk to you, Ruthie."

It seemed important so I responded, "Okay."

He then said with greater emotion, "Meet me on the front porch after supper, Ruthie."

I answered with some curiosity, "Okay, I'll be there."

Later, on the front porch, George stood before me, speaking words I had longed to hear: "Will you marry me, Ruthie?"

My response was, "Give me a couple of days to pray about it." I could not believe I had responded in such a manner! I had already prayed plenty about this before he ever asked me the question. We had never gone on a date nor had we conversed alone, except when he first arrived on campus and I had shown him around. I had cut his hair a few times, just as I had done for other men on campus. It was a complete surprise for George to ask me such an important question.

After the couple of days I had asked for, I gave him my answer: "I will marry you because I am sure you are the one for me as I have prayed much about it." He gave me a quick, shy kiss and we each went back to our dorms. George later told me that I was the first girl he had ever kissed. George was forty years old and had never been kissed and had never even gone out with a girl. I, Ruthie Morrow had the special privilege of being the first and only girl to receive his favor.

Our dating consisted mostly of sitting together in class. Then, George became very sick with rheumatoid arthritis. It became so severe that he was bedridden for more than a month. As he began to recuperate enough to be able to walk with the use of a cane, we decided to set a date for the wedding. It was to take place in my hometown of East Springfield, Pennsylvania. Dr. P. H. Augustine would marry us in the Federated Church, the church I had attended in my childhood, next door to my family's home.

A wedding gown was lent to me and George borrowed a dark blue suit to wear for our special day. The day before the wedding, George had asked me if there was anything in particular I wanted of him for our wedding day. My answer to him was, "Could you please walk in the church for the ceremony without the cane?" The next day, October 24, 1955, George walked into the church without the cane. He had decided that he would do his best never to use that cane again.

George and I returned to language school as husband and wife. We enjoyed studying about how languages were formed. We were taught how to listen to the sounds that form words, and then put those sounds into writing, and finally translate them. This would be of great help to us as missionaries.

It was during our language studies that we discovered we

were going to become parents. Louise, our beautiful little girl, was born on July 31, 1956. George now began to think about going through customs with his family. He did not want us to be separated from each other as had happened when he had entered the United States. American citizens were placed in one line and non-American citizens in another. To solve this problem, George decided I should obtain British citizenship. We went to the British Consulate in Chicago and I completed the application. Just before signing the papers, I asked, "Do I lose my American citizenship?" The gentleman's answer was in these exact words: "No, you just jeopardize it." I thought I would have to be a criminal or commit some drastic deed to lose my citizenship. I made the decision to sign the paperwork and was led to believe that I now had dual citizenship.

When our language studies were completed in 1957, we were commissioned as missionaries, ready to go wherever the Lord led us to serve Him. Now we began the preliminary work of gathering items that would aid us on the field. A high chair that had been in a fire was donated to us. After determining that it was only covered in smoke and not actually damaged, we scrubbed it and gave it a new coat of paint. Making a trip to Chicago to visit a missionary supply house, we added a projector that used a candle to show pictures and a James washer, a u-shaped tub with a hand-worked agitator. So many other items were donated that it became necessary for a large wooden crate to be built for shipping everything to our new destination.

During this busy preparation time, George and I did not have many opportunities to share our burden in churches. As a result, we went to the field with only $150.00 monthly to supply the needs of three people. The Lord never failed us. He always supplied our needs, often in unexpected ways.

We were asked by the mission leaders to consider going to Bolivia. There we would be working in a school for missionaries' children. George and I both immediately felt a peace and were very sure this was what we were to do. We instantly said, "Yes."

Paperwork would be a priority. First, we applied for passports. We were so excited when those passports arrived in the mail! The arrival of the passports seemed to make our dreams of the mission field become more real. Visas for Bolivia had to be applied for and approved. The visas were granted, taking us another step forward in our journey to take the gospel to those who had never heard the good news. Such excitement we felt, especially when plans were made for the big wooden crate to be sent on its way to Cochabamba, Bolivia.

We were ready to begin the long voyage by ocean liner to Antofagasta, Chile, followed by a two-day train trip and then a week in Cochabamba to finish our paperwork. After a seven-hour Galgo (Spanish for Greyhound) bus ride to Tambo, we would be through traveling and could at last get involved in the work God had planned for us to do in Bolivia.

CHAPTER THREE

LED

"...He calls His own sheep by name and leads them out."
John 10:3

There was nothing but excitement and joy as we prepared to follow God into this new chapter of our lives. In November 1957, the Burt family sailed from the docks of New York City on the QUEEN ELIZABETH, the ocean liner which would take us to England. Every day brought us closer to George's homeland where we expected to arrive in early December.

The two months we spent in England were filled with visits with family and friends and with many opportunities to share about our future work in Bolivia. Getting acquainted with my new relatives was a pleasure, and I began to feel that I had truly become a part of the family. George and I were able to speak in three churches while we were there, enabling us to share with others about where God was leading us and about the work to be done in our soon-to-be home, Tambo, Bolivia.

George, Louise and I said our goodbyes and sailed from Southampton, England, to continue our journey to our ultimate destination, our place of service. We now headed for Antofagasta, Chile, wondering what awaited us there. Sailing on the REINA

DEL MAR, Spanish for QUEEN OF THE OCEAN, was very interesting with stops in many fascinating ports along the way.

One port that provided the source for much discussion and thought was Cuba. As the ship docked there, George and I noted the influences of Castro's takeover of Cuba's government. Armed men were everywhere. We dared not relax and we felt unable to enjoy the people or surroundings to the fullest. It seemed to us that if we even tramped on a blade of grass at the edge of the sidewalk, we would be in trouble.

Leaving Cuba, we continued toward the Panama Canal which we both found especially interesting. Our eyes were wide open, observing everything about the workings of this magnificent design of man that aids the economy and travel of the world. Passing through the canal, we found ourselves sailing into the Pacific Ocean heading south. Feelings of being nearer our destination filled our hearts, while our brains told us there was still a long distance to travel as the ship moved slowly down the western coast of South America.

As the REINA DEL MAR passed the coast of Venezuela, a group of young men came swimming toward us. These South American natives had learned the English word, "money." They had developed the habit of swimming out near incoming ships to attract the attention of the assumed-to-be-rich passengers by crying out, "Money, money, money!" The excited passengers would respond by throwing coins to them. Quickly, the natives disappeared beneath the beautiful blue-green ocean water, reappearing minutes later with the retrieved coins. As George, Louise and I watched the young men surface several times after diving for coins, we were fascinated to see that their cheeks had become their storage pouches, bulging with coins and reminding us of little chipmunks.

Though the stops seemed to slow us down and to keep us from the place we longed to be, we knew these delays offered new opportunities to learn the ways of different cultures. We had been given the opportunity to dock at Colombia, British Guiana, Venezuela, Ecuador and Peru, each stop providing us new insights into the cultures of those among whom we would soon be living. After six weeks on board the REINA DEL MAR, we docked at our last port-of-call, Antofagasta, Chile.

From the ship, George and I saw a train which had recently departed Antofagasta and was now making its arduous way up a nearby mountain. We soon learned that this was the train that made only one journey each week from Antofagasta, Chile, to Cochabamba, Bolivia. We had no choice but to wait to continue our travels.

Previous arrangements had been made for us to stay at the Salvation Army Home in Antofagasta. We planned to use our week's delay for walking in the area, not only to help us learn more about Chile but also to help make the days pass more quickly. We noticed that due to a shortage of rain for several years, everything- land, animals, plants, even people- appeared to be extremely dry. We were soon to discover that this dryness brought undesirable guests, which in turn brought George a test of faith concerning our missionary service.

When we awoke the first morning after arriving in Antofagasta, we found that the house was full of fleas. Overnight, they had made their presence so painfully apparent that George was tempted to leave missions. All of us, including little Louise, were covered with painful bites. Horrible memories of living with fleas during the war rushed to George's mind. He could hardly bare to see his baby looking as if she had measles, and the certainty that more bites awaited her prompted him to say, "Ruthie, I think we need to go back home. I just can't stand Louise getting bitten up so much by fleas." He could accept it for himself but not for his baby.

I quickly responded, "You can't waste the money people

have given to get us here only to turn around and go back home. I'm not going back just because of fleas." This sounded rather harsh, but it helped George realize that we had committed our lives to the Lord and to the work in Bolivia and we must continue by faith, fleas or no fleas.

Commitment would keep us here, but it would not rid us of the fleas and their torment. Like us, they were here to stay. They were not only in the home but, due to the dryness, in the streets as well. Each time we walked outside, at the top of my ankle socks would appear a little black circle of fleas- not the best jewelry to brag about to your friends. The Salvation Army, while a great asset for our family, could offer us assistance in many ways, but even they could not rid us of those fleas.

When the time came, our kind Salvation Army friends went with George to book our tickets for Cochabamba, Bolivia. Then when departure time arrived, they took us to the train station. We would travel approximately two days to reach Cochabamba, and I just knew we were headed for even more wonderful experiences with God's blessings in the form of gifted, loving people. Through the people God provided, we were growing to see how He places individuals and experiences in His children's lives at just the right moment to bless and teach those whose hearts are dedicated to going forth in His Name.

The train on which we had arranged to travel was assembled in an unusual way. At the front of the train were the cars which transported people who had paid a standard fee. The next group of cars were the sleeper cars. After the sleeper cars were the cars with no seats and then the dining car. To be fair, different fees had been charged for the cars with different accommodations, but all must pass through the "no seat" car to eat their meals in the dining car.

Since we had started our travel early Saturday morning and would not arrive at our destination until late Sunday night, we travelled in a sleeper car. As we entered the car with no seats, we were met by a burst of sound. There were the sounds of mothers gently humming to their crying babies as they rocked them back and forth. There was random laughter and conversation between the people who were sharing the limited space. George and I could hardly hear one another. Many people were standing, some amid baggage, crates and boxes. Others were sitting on the floor. Occasionally, a passenger had to climb over someone lying in the floor attempting to sleep.

As the train wound its way up through the mountains, we began to relax and take in the changing scenery. We noted the plant life beginning to look very dry, and then, as we traveled across the high desert area, we saw almost no plant life at all. We were overwhelmed with all that there was to see and tried to absorb as much as we could. We talked very little, until it grew dark, limiting what we could see. Until time to turn in for the night, we shared a delightful time of exchanging our many observations and thoughts about what we had seen during the day.

We had just settled in, and at about midnight, a knock was heard at the door of our sleeper car. When we sleepily answered the knock, the official-looking person at the door asked for our passports since we were about to enter the country of Bolivia. Early the next morning, the passports were returned to us and we found that we were still in the desert which stretched straight into Bolivia.

After getting ourselves ready for the day, we began making our way through the no seat car to the dining car. Then, after finishing the meal, it was time for the challenge to return to our car- all for a simple meal. Returning to our seats, our eyes were once again fixed on the changing scenes that appeared at the window.

After traveling through the dry and dusty desert for many

hours, we noticed a greater change. We were finally descending out of the mountain heights. After seeing very few houses during the first portion of the journey, we were excited now to see a house come into view and then, fifteen minutes later, another. Our excitement was rapidly building as we sensed the end of our journey drawing near.

More and more homes appeared in our view from the train windows. We now saw small villages with people and animals. One would have thought George and I were about to enter a grand city with all the emotion we were feeling and expressing as the train continued down the mountain. As we considered that we were going to the very place Almighty God had chosen for us, no grander city could be found.

We still faced two more times of struggle to reach the dining car, but these were successfully accomplished. During those last miles, it was as if God knew how our hearts yearned to arrive at our last stop and He permitted the train greater speed. The sun had towered in the sky producing beautiful shades of red, pink and yellow, but now the sky was darkening, and the train reached an even lower altitude where more and more villages appeared. Soon the train entered the City of Cochabama, altitude 8,392 feet. We had arrived! We were in Cochabamba, Bolivia!

Somewhat nervous, we wondered where we would go from here. George looked at me and said, "I hope someone is here to meet us!" Everyone else on the train began getting their luggage ready to disembark. There was chatter coming from all directions as people waited to be told they could leave the train. Through the open windows, we now heard someone speaking English. Our hearts skipped a few beats as we listened closely. We could not believe our ears for we recognized the voices. With great delight I said, "It sounds like Evelyne and Dan!"

How those voices encouraged us! When we had no idea where the mission house was, Evelyne and Dan with whom we had studied in our language classes were here to help us find our way. They introduced us to all the missionaries, and we recalled that we had prayed for many of them in the past. Our hearts were so full of joy as God now gave us the privilege of meeting them in person.

Another special surprise was waiting for us when we arrived at our room. Opening the doors to the small, clean room, we were totally taken aback to see a bed and a chair. I had expected to go where I would have nothing, and my God had exceeded my expectations. He had provided for our comfort by giving us not only a bed but also a chair! With a grateful heart, I exclaimed for all to hear, "There is a chair! We have a chair, too!" God had supplied so graciously as He led us to the land where we were to serve Him and now was abundantly providing for all our needs there. How we rejoiced in our God!

The next morning, refreshed after a good night's rest and a filling breakfast, George and I were ready for the challenge of paperwork. The mission field director of Bolivia served as our guide about the City of Cochabamba, beginning at the government offices which would become our "home away from home." For a full week, we spent many hours going from one office to another, completing the paperwork required to remain in the country. With each new demand, we grew more eager to be on our way.

We were becoming progressively aware of cultural differences. In the city, when a car approached an intersection, the driver would honk his horn and keep going without a stop. The person who honked first had the understood right of way and the other cars were supposed to stop. But we wondered, what if two- or even more than two- cars happened to honk at the same time?

The busy week in Cochabamba seemed to be never-ending, but when it finally came to its conclusion, we had our official

Bolivian identification and residential papers in hand. We were on our way to Tambo, our long-awaited place of service.

Now that we were nearing the end of our long journey, we reflected on God's provision through His people, specifically the people of the Federated Church in East Springfield who had supplied our travel expenses. He also provided through "Mom Jenofsky," an older lady who had served in Bolivia and who now came to travel with us in order to help us with the language and culture adjustments.

Starting bright and early in the morning, the four of us now boarded the only bus traveling in our direction that day, bound for Santa Cruz. Our destination, Tambo, was about two-thirds of the way to Santa Cruz. Traveling through the country area, George and I were, as usual, busy staring out the windows, intently absorbing everything we saw. Due to the chilling temperatures at these high desert altitudes, there was little vegetation. The buildings were built with mud brick (adobe) and were scattered quite a distance from each other. I remarked to George, "Look, we can see the round things on the houses like we saw on the houses in the desert of Chile."

We soon learned about those round things from Mom Jenofsky. They were storage units for fuel used to heat the homes. Wood was not readily available, so the need for fuel was met by using a substance that was available in abundance: cow pies. Dried cow pies were gathered and stored on their houses. When needed, they burned well and provided heat for the homes.

Mom had a speech impediment which was occasionally awkward, but she was delightful and very kind to us. She was very knowledgeable about the area and its people, and we gleaned as much as we could as she talked. She told us that the people were very hard-working and were descendants of the Incans. She cautioned us never to judge a book by its cover because, though many of the people might appear to be poor due to their manner of dress, they were a proud people and were known to have money saved for emergencies. They were also careful not to give an appearance of wealth. In the mountains, clean water was not always available for washing clothes or for taking a bath, so body odor and dirty clothing often resulted.

We also learned about the sheep we had noticed grazing in the surrounding areas. The sheep were raised for their wool that would be sheared and woven into wool yarn which would be used to make skirts, pants, shirts and hats. These woolen items provided the warmth needed in this cold mountainous region where even summer temperatures often ran in the fifties and sixties.

Families with money often bought a young boy to serve as a shepherd. These boys, usually between the ages of nine and eleven, could be seen dotting the hillsides, caring for the sheep and protecting them from predators. Young girls could also be bought to serve in the household to do cleaning.

We had now been traveling almost three hours and our bus pulled over and stopped at a large building. George and I continued to sit, as if in school, listening to Mom Jenofsky explain how the people used the sun to tell time. I was listening intently, but I was also watching the activity taking place outside the bus. Passengers who had disembarked were now mingling with the black-haired, dark-eyed natives and were buying bread and other items. Some were buying fried fish from women who were warmly dressed in wool skirts. The fish still had their heads, fins and tails, but the internal organs had been removed. As we left the bus and walked among the people, we noticed that some of those who were selling their wares were very shrewd and not altogether honest. Some of them had nails taped in hidden areas on their scales; some intentionally miscounted the number of items purchased. Buyer beware!

I turned my attention to the people and their clothing. The men wore wool pants. The pants had two flaps which overlapped in front and the waist was then rolled down to secure the flaps. No belt was used. They wore shoes made from old tires. They simply cut out the shoes in a continuous pattern and then tied this on to their feet.

The women wore dark wool skirts, saving their bright-colored clothes for festivals and special occasions. They all wore their dark hair in two braids tied together at the back of their heads. Between the two braids was a black piece of yarn from which other strands of wool hung, each strand representing one child. This was a practical hair style with the hair held out of the way while they cooked or worked. All the women worked at keeping house, cooking, and bearing children. Female children were undesirable and considered extra mouths to feed. Such darkness fills the hearts of those who have not experienced the love of Christ!

I noticed some people drifting behind a large building and saw that the men went to one side while the women went to the other. Having seen no restroom facilities, I assumed I understood the separate movements of the people, but I decided to ask Mom to avoid an embarrassing situation. As I prepared to leave the bus to stretch my aching muscles and take care of personal needs, I asked her for advice. Her response: "You do-do-do-do as they do or do-do-don't do." In spite of her speech impediment, I understood, and we moved in the direction of the large building.

Young missionaries often find themselves in "culture shock" as they face situations for which they have not been prepared. The conveniences of home may not be available in the place of service, and new solutions and methods will be necessary. This was now our experience as we moved to the back of the building where we had observed men and women walking to opposite sides. No facilities or restrooms were in sight, there were very few small bushes for privacy, and, to make matters worse, I had worn a straight skirt! Now was certainly the time for new solutions and methods! I faced my personal culture shock and re-boarded the bus, thankful that God had used even the long journey to Tambo as a training ground for our new life of service among the Quecha people.

As we traveled from an altitude of approximately 12,000 feet to an elevation of about 5,000 feet, more vegetation came into view. We knew we were getting closer to our destination. Mom was a true comfort, answering all our questions and reassuring us whenever we were confused. Louise was a wonderful traveler and was content throughout the journey. We were thankful that she had been entertained the entire trip by gazing out the window as I held her.

There were still several hours of travel ahead of us- long hours that would be spent winding around, up and down in the Andes Mountains. It was not unusual to see on the steep mountainside, a dark-haired man stooped over with a shovel or hoe in hand, working a field of potatoes. No modern machinery could be used on such steep mountainsides. Now the bus began its slow steady descent, and more trees, bushes, shrubs, and even a cactus appeared as we entered the foothills of the Andes Mountains. Soon, the bus stopped in the town of Camarapa where we received the good news that our destination was not very far away now. Then, at last, we were in Tambo, our home for the first term in the field.

CHAPTER FOUR

SERVING

"It is the Lord Christ Whom you serve."
Colossians 3:24

Tambo means "resting place." Located about two-thirds of the way from Cochabamba to Santa Cruz, Tambo had indeed become a resting place for many people journeying by donkey or horse. The river there provided a place to water animals, bathe, cook, or wash clothes as weary travelers rested for a day or two before continuing their travel.

Tambo was now owned by the New Tribes Mission and was used as a boarding school for the children of missionaries. The intention was to provide schooling for the children, freeing the parents from teaching their children at home, allowing them more time to concentrate on their work with the Bolivian people.

We arrived in Tambo and were filled with joy as we gathered our baggage and prepared to make our final departure from the bus. Mom Jenofsky would also be working at Tambo, and I looked forward to continued fellowship with this special lady. We were greeted by enthusiastic students and staff, and after greetings and introductions, two of the men took our suitcases and led us to our new residence.

Our living quarters consisted of a bedroom for George and me and a smaller room for Louise. We were to be dorm parents to boys in grades one through eight and would share a living room with the boys. As we looked about our new home, we suddenly realized that we were actually here- with fourteen boys and little time to familiarize ourselves with this new world in which we had come to serve. We were overwhelmed and delighted at the same time.

Our first priority was to get acquainted with our new home and work area. We began by walking the grounds. We noticed that a fence enclosed the buildings at Tambo which were laid out in a rectangular shape. The classes were held in the end of one of the buildings; the kitchen, dining room and auditorium were in the other end. The boys' and girls' dorms were positioned along each side. The restrooms were separate buildings behind each dorm. Other buildings, including the food pantry, laundry area, and workshop, were located behind the kitchen area. There was no electricity in the area, but the school had a generator to supply all the buildings with light.

A system had been arranged for meeting the needs of operating the mission. Quechua people from the surrounding area came to the gate to sell produce, thus supplying the school with fresh vegetables. Other items such as food staples and office supplies were ordered by two-way radio and received from either Cochabamba or Santa Cruz.

To help with the upkeep of the grounds and buildings, each student had a work detail assignment. These work details took place after classes were dismissed for the day. The children watered the hanging plants around the patio buildings, swept assigned areas, cleaned classrooms, and did other tasks to help the staff. The children did not seem to mind doing these assignments, and, in fact, seemed to take pride in performing them well.

George and I had much to learn and many adjustments to make, but we were encouraged by God's command to "fight the good fight of faith" (1 Timothy 6:12). Experienced missionaries patiently answered our many questions, and we were willing and eager to learn. One of our challenges was learning how to handle the dorm situation. Although some of the children's parents were with other mission boards in places as far away as Brazil and Venezuela, most of them were missionaries with New Tribes Mission. This gave our dorm an interesting and challenging blend of personalities, beliefs and behaviors.

In addition to our duties as dorm parents, we also taught classes. George and I made the important decision that one of us would always remain at home with our little Louise while the other taught the required classes. George taught history, a subject he especially loved, to students in grades five through eight. I chose to teach a couple of other subjects to grades five through six. I added first and second grades the following year when another teacher left the classroom after the birth of a new baby.

Every weekday after the first morning bell, some of the children practiced piano in the auditorium. Our bedroom was very near the auditorium, so every morning, we heard the same notes and the same chords over and over again. After a while, the constant repetition grated on my nerves. I reminded myself that the children had to practice if they were to perfect their skills to someday bless the world with the beauty of music. This reminder did help a little, but the best remedy for a particularly repetitious morning was cotton for plugging the ears.

I spent my days with some dear children. Most of them were gentle, obedient, and kind, but there were some mischievous ones and a few who had bad tempers. Each one was God's child and needed to be trained to walk in His ways. I took this task to heart and worked diligently to meet each child's individual needs.

While teaching grades five and six, I had to face the "new teacher challenge." All new teachers must meet this challenge in order to prove worthy of respect, and I was no exception. Peter was the one student brave enough to offer the "behind the teacher's back challenge." Each time I approached the blackboard and turned my back to write, snickering began. In spite of my cautioning, this disruptive behavior continued. I ordered the behavior to stop immediately, knowing full well it would be up to me to catch and stop the culprit. The next time I heard the snickering begin, I whirled around quickly and caught Peter with his next scheme in progress. Red-faced and ashamed, the boy who had thought he had the upperhand of the teacher was dismissed from the classroom. Waiting for the class to end afforded time for Peter to wonder what horrible punishment he might receive, and, at last, he was escorted to the principal's office. In the days that followed, the word went out, "Do not mess with Mrs. Burt. She spanks really hard." The stalemate was over. The warming up of his "seat of understanding" had established my authority as a teacher.

We also faced challenges at home. One of the boys in our dorm had a terrible temper and would sometimes threaten other children with a knife. We needed wisdom from our Lord for a solution to this problem. After much prayer, George decided to respond with punishment every time he threw a temper tantrum, even if no one else was threatened. Being consistent paid off and eventually the temper tantrums ceased. Years later, that young man thanked George for helping him to overcome this defect of his character.

Each day began with a wakeup call at 6:30 a.m. and was immediately followed by the chattering of children as they dressed and got ready for school. One cute little first grade boy with dark, curly hair struggled to get ready on time in the morning's rush of chaos. After a while, we realized that Donald did not know how to tie his shoes. His missionary parents worked in Santa Cruz and had not yet had the opportunity to teach him this skill. George became the boy's buddy and his patient, loving attention soon resulted in Donald dressing himself independently, tying his own shoes, and getting ready on time.

As I watched my husband in his service to God and observed his obvious insight into the hearts of the children, I discovered that a man's strength never shines forth so clearly as in his humble, gentle acts. George's interaction with the children was a visible expression of his commitment to God's way: "The Lord's bondservant must not be quarrelsome, but be kind to all, able to teach, patient when wronged, with gentleness correcting those who are in opposition" 2 Timothy 2:24-25.

Our second child was born January 10, 1959. With her beautiful curly hair, Rebecca looked like a little doll. We were overjoyed with our new addition, as were all the children and staff. We continued with our plan for one of us to care for our children while the other was working.

The daily routine for the staff and students was well established. After school, all the children fifth grade and up started faithfully on their work detail which was then followed by free time until the supper bell rang. Sometimes there was another free time after supper. If homework was not completed, the students had about an hour of study hall. Everyone was then expected back in the dorm by a certain time, dressed in their pajamas, ready for evening devotions in the living room. While the boys prepared for devotions, I helped our two girls get ready for bed. After group devotions, everyone crawled into bed for a good night's sleep. For little ones (grades one through four), bedtime was at 8:30 in the evening. Grades five through eight had a curfew of 9:30 and high schoolers turned in at 10:00. The generator was turned off at 10:30 every night and all was quiet in the Tambo dorms.

On Saturdays, my role changed from that of teacher to barber. Most Saturday mornings, I was kept busy cutting hair for all the boys. Flat tops were quite popular even on the mission field, and this style required real skill to cut.

Each Sunday provided an opportunity for an uplifting church service followed by a delicious lunch. The afternoon was a free time for all to enjoy. Our little family often took pleasant evening strolls together in the quiet evening air, a special time of unity for us as a family.

One of our added responsibilities at school was to take turns filling in for the cook to allow that hardworking missionary a day of rest. I confess that I did not welcome my designated Sunday. I could think of many things I would rather do during those long hours of preparing the vegetables and meats for cooking and serving, and I was so glad when the day was over.

Our coworkers Dr. James Black and his wife Lois served in the little girls' dorm. Dr. Black was an Englishman, which delighted George, and he cared for the medical needs of the student body and those of the Quechua people in the area. The Blacks were preparing to go to Argentina to work with college students. After several months of working together as dorm parents, Dr. Black surprised me by asking if I would consider taking his job of being responsible for medical needs. I stood in absolute shock. I could not believe what I was hearing. I had always been interested in medical work, but I had taken only one medical course and it was about only the most basic health needs. How could Dr. Black think I could assume so great a responsibility? After regaining some ability to reason, I told him, "No, I can't do it." Fear washed over me- fear of my lack of knowledge, fear of harming someone, fear of taking on a task too great for me. Fear is often the great enemy to God's will, and it was now hindering my commitment to God's work.

George and I began to pray for God's wisdom. As we waited for God's leading, we acknowledged that God was stretching us beyond our human ability. It would be He and He alone who would perform the task. We would obey in faith and trust Him to guide and provide. "Do not fear, for I am with you; do not anxiously look about you, for I am your God. I will strengthen you, surely I will help you, surely I will uphold you with My righteous hand" Isaiah 41:10. This became my verse of encouragement.

Before going to the mission field, a nurse friend had given me all her nursing books. At the time, I wondered why she chose to give them to a girl with no medical training. The gift of nursing books before I knew I would need them was God's provision for the plan He had already chosen for my life. George made it possible for me to study and work, and as I found time to read through those books, I gained new knowledge each day.

After Dr. Black left, word about "La Señora Rut" spread quickly. I was now the one to see for help with all sorts of medical needs. George was always ready to care for our children in order to free me to attend the people. He always tried to arrange for someone to see me safely to the patient's home at night if he could not go with me himself. I became the envy of many when I received my very own bicycle, a treasure on the mission field. Blessings be upon the giver, for prior to receiving this wonderful gift, I made many long and difficult treks to the homes of my patients.

As I visited in Quechua homes, I became aware of the unsanitary conditions in which they lived and of many customs which were harmful to their health in ways they did not realize. The need for greater prayer and dependence on God's wisdom and guidance was more apparent than ever. I would need to be in constant contact with God if I were to be effective in this ministry. I was very careful not to do anything to offend the people, and I respected their customs as much as I could. This required me to grow in my understanding of their behaviors, customs and beliefs, and I continually sought God's wisdom and His guiding insights. As Paul directed in 2 Corinthians 6:3-10, "... giving no cause for offense in anything, so that the ministry will not be discredited, but in everything commending ourselves as servants of God..."

Our first Christmas on the field, we made our own decorations since there were not many available in the stores in Cochabamba. We cut long slender strips from a tin can, twisted them to make icicles and hung them on a tree we had cut down. There were little pods all over its branches, but we didn't mind since we liked the shape of the tree. It was an absolute delightful surprise when the pods opened, resulting in puffs of snowy white cotton all over the branches. Our Christmas tree had made its own unbelievably gorgeous decorations! We shared our beautiful tree in the school auditorium where there would be a Christmas service for the people who stayed behind during the two-week school break.

Near the end of the school year, it was customary for the children to put on a play for all the parents who would be arriving from their mission stations all over the country. This night was a special night for students, parents and teachers. The children, excited and anxious to impress their parents, practiced diligently to learn their parts. There were three drama performances, one by each age group of students. Throughout the grade school performance, chuckles of delight were heard, a common sound when little children grace a stage and parents are so proud of their little darlings. The high school play was much longer, taking the whole evening to present in a very professional manner. The parents and staff were pleased, and all thoroughly enjoyed the presentation. The conclusion of this time of togetherness was graduation on the final night before everyone left for summer vacation.

Did I hear the word *vacation*? I am not sure George and I ever discovered that word's true meaning. In addition to all the other tasks of home, studying Spanish was another duty that required time during the three-month school vacation. This study was necessary to help us converse more fluently with the nationals, creating greater avenues for ministry. I managed to complete a two-year course in three months. George, on the other hand, found language studies to be difficult, but he worked very hard and completed the one-year course.

South American schools were in session from April to just before Christmas, but our school at Tambo kept the same schedule as schools in the United States. Regardless of the schedule, the vacation time was never long enough. It seemed that we had just had graduation and begun our three months of Spanish studies, and it was already time to start a new school year. As the children returned to Tambo, the routine was much the same as the year before. I would continue caring for the medical needs of the students and of the people of the outlying villages in addition to my responsibilities at school and at home.

The wind often grew strong in the afternoon and swirls of dust and dirt were lifted from the ground and carried along to be dumped somewhere else. It seemed to me that our dorm was that wind's dumping station. Since there was a screen door on our building, we left the solid door open to allow air to circulate through the screen into the house. Because of this, it seemed I was always dusting the sala, the living room, at least twice every afternoon. It had to be done often to keep "dust messages" from being written all over the furniture.

I have always liked plants and flowers, and one day as I was caring for some plants at the end of our dorm, Mom Jenofsky brought me a stick of poinsettia plant saying, "Ruthie, let's stick it in the ground and see if it will grow." I responded, "Ok, let's do it," putting it in the ground right then. Over the next few days, I watered the stick some but did not give it any special care. After a short time, I observed the stick develop into a beautiful flowering two-foot-tall plant. By the next year, it had reached over three feet tall and had produced twenty-seven large beautiful flowers. It was a mass of red beauty. This was a gorgeous gift from God, especially since at our altitude of 5,000 feet, we experienced freezing temperatures during the winter.

Many different types of cacti grew in the area. One morning when George and I woke early, we looked out the window and were greeted by a breathtaking sight of beautiful, large white flowers which had opened on the cacti that covered the hill behind the girls' dorm. That night as the sinking sun moved slowly amid a cascade of color, the cacti were silhouetted beautifully in the foreground, just for our pleasure it seemed.

The children enjoyed playing on a nearby mountain which they called White Mountain. The name was appropriate because the mountain seemed lighter in appearance than the surrounding area probably due to mica in the soil. There were many small gullies and dense bushes scattered here and there, providing many convenient hiding places for their games. This was the ideal place to gather on a good moonlit night to play "Steal the Flag." Summer evenings were very pleasant, comfortable enough to go without a sweater. One such night, George and I were invited to join the fun, but George opted out, leaving me to face my opponents all alone- without adult help, that is. The children excitedly taught me the basic rules, stressing the all-important one that under absolutely no circumstance were you to allow yourself to be caught. Being the new kid on the block and a teacher at that, I knew I would be the designated target. Mindful of the objective of not being caught, I took off running to avoid capture. Noticing what appeared to be a good, level landing spot, I leaped upward and out into the moonlit night to make my escape. Suddenly, I found myself unable to breathe. As I had made my jump, my knees had hit my chest so hard that the wind was knocked out of me. I had not been caught, even though judging distance in the moonlight was very deceiving. The kids and I were delighted in our play on White Mountain and made many memories that I will always cherish.

A river located near the back of the school property provided fun for the students on Saturdays. There were shallow places where the small children could wade and play safely. The older children could dive and swim in deeper water.

In addition to playing on White Mountain and in the river, the children found amusement in the simplest of things. In the dorms, all clothing was marked, and a day was assigned for each dorm's laundry to be washed. The boys' dorm had a laundry basket large enough to accommodate all their stinky outfits. One afternoon, one of the boys was sick in bed and was starting to feel bored when he was surprised to see a chicken strut into the room. Timmy watched as the chicken walked over to the laundry basket, climbed in, and made herself quite at home. Timmy waited and watched intently and was delighted when the chicken stood up, revealing an egg! Timmy spent the rest of the day, watching the chicken and hoping for a repeat performance. His "chicken delight" had transformed a boring sick day.

Entertaining the children required a variety of games and entertainment. The little boys loved the competition of marbles and so did our little Rebecca. Our little baby who looked like a doll with all her curls now loved to join the boys as they played marbles. Louise loved playing with a rag doll that I had made for her. Later, her play companion was a Chatty Cathy doll. Both Louise and Rebecca loved playing outdoors. The older boys enjoyed becoming experts with their weapon of choice, slingshots. I guess rain must be mentioned as well, for it seemed that every time it rained, the kids always enjoyed playing in the puddles. We watched the children closely and didn't allow them to play near any of the school's gates after a concerned neighbor told us that one of the nationals planned to steal Rebecca. We thanked the Lord that the kidnapping plan never came to pass.

Sometimes entertainment came as a result of mispronunciation. One day our neighbor, Señora Antoñia was with me in our living room as I was cutting out a dress for Louise. Señora Antoñia wanted to cut out a piece of material herself so I let her, telling her to cut it an inch longer in Spanish. She erupted into laughter immediately, later explaining that I had said, "Cut it a flea longer." In Spanish, the word for *flea* is *pulga* and the word for *inch* is *pulgada*. On another occasion, one of the missionaries found that while he thought he was preaching on sin (pecado), he was actually giving a sermon on fish (pescado).

The school children did not suffer from the same serious medical issues as the native children. Among our students, the most serious complaints were headaches, stomachaches, fevers, and occasional sprained ankles and wrists. From time to time, I was faced with a disease of the imagination, usually suffered by those who wished to stay in bed to escape an exam. This disease had to be treated quickly to prevent its spread to other students. In one case, two boys I'll call Steve and Tom decided to visit the castor bean bushes that grew near the school and consume just enough to develop a reaction that would allow them to miss a dreaded test. Well, they did have a reaction, but it was far more serious than the one they expected. Castor beans are poisonous, and the boys became seriously ill. Thankfully, they were able to sleep off the negative effects and were back to normal later the same day. In spite of their best efforts, they still had to take the test, and they had also learned an important lesson.

I was often called into the nearby community for the treatment of dysentery, anemia, and intestinal parasites, conditions often caused by or worsened by a lack of sanitary conditions. There were also calls to treat snake bites and insect bites, including bites from the nigua, a burrowing sand flea that lays its eggs under the skin of the foot. I attended all who called, whether the complaint was a severe wound or an abnormal pregnancy.

In order to provide affordable care, I charged only for the cost of the medical items used. I could deliver a baby at home for only ten cents! If my patients had no money, they paid with eggs or poultry. At different times, I received a chick, a baby turkey, and a mature chicken. Sometimes I was given corn, fish or bread. The people were grateful and always gave something to help pay for the cost of the supplies used for their care.

I was eventually registered in Bolivia as a sanitaria (health officer) which gave me the authority to purchase medical supplies and to treat people in any outlying area at my discretion. I was not authorized to work in the city, but I did not mind that restriction since I was interested in serving those who did not already have access to medical help.

The day came when I was called to deliver my first baby. I was very concerned. Would I do everything right? "Calm down," I told myself. "Who is always by my side to provide help and wisdom? My all-sufficient Lord!" I hurried to the village home with my missionary friend Ellen Parker, and we planned and rehearsed procedures as we walked. The delivery went according to plan and resulted in the birth of a beautiful healthy baby and a mother in good condition. Mother and baby continued to do well, and I was flooded with gratitude as I realized that I was truly in God's hands and that He would use me to reveal Himself to those for whom I provided medical care.

Soon, La Señora Rut needed medical care herself. I had

been having some health difficulties for several months and now I had an ongoing fever. George and the field staff decided that my condition demanded the difficult travel by bus to Cochabamba to be examined by a trained doctor. It rained all day as I traveled to the hospital. Now I arrived at this place of supposed health and healing and found myself staring at mud. Thick, gooey mud was everywhere, and no one seemed to be concerned about cleaning it up.

The doctor who examined me determined that my tonsils must be removed. In South America at that time, it was the practice for a patient to purchase any required medical supplies themselves. The doctor now gave me a list of the things he would require for my surgery: local anesthesia, stitching, antibiotics, etc. The next morning, I returned to the hospital for the surgery and presented the medical supplies to the doctor. He directed me to an old iron chair and told me to sit down and open my mouth as wide as possible. As I tried to comply, he moved toward me and began rapidly injecting Novocain from one point to another all over the back of my throat. It did not take long for the anesthesia to take effect.

A short time later, I woke to find the doctor and another man lifting me from the chair. As the bed for surgery was not yet ready for me, I was to be placed on the muddy floor to wait. Without thinking, I had worn my wardrobe enemy, a straight cut dress, and it now slid up and over my hips. I was unable to adjust it and the men made no effort to stop in the task of moving me- so much for modesty. During the move, I couldn't help but notice that with every step the men took, big clods of mud were falling off their shoes. This certainly didn't encourage much confidence in the sanitary conditions for my surgery. When at last I was placed on a bed, I was relieved to be able to get my dress back in place before the operation began. I was awake and able to watch as the doctor removed my tonsils.

Following the surgery, I was guided to another bed where I rested for about half an hour. The doctor then returned to check for bleeding. Thankfully, there was none, so he said to me, "Now, you can go home." A message was radioed to Tambo to inform George that the surgery was completed. One of the missionaries would come to take me home, and I waited two days before traveling back to Tambo. My healing progressed with no infection and I was once again thankful for God's protective hand.

Things returned to normal, and a few days later, I faced an unexpected challenge. A native lady in labor had walked more than a mile to receive La Señora Rut's help. Expecting a typical delivery, I began an exam. When I checked the lady, to my astonishment, I discovered the baby's right arm was already extending from the mother's body. This meant that the baby was now in a cross-section position and must be turned. I called on the Lord for help and proceeded to cleanse the mother and the little arm. When I was sure that everything was sanitized, I began to gently ease the arm back into place as the mother's pain lessened. Now it was necessary to position the baby such that the head would be directed downward. This would require me to reach into the birth canal to rotate the little body. Once this was done, the baby's head was in place and the little one could be born with no difficulty. Their lives were no longer in danger. How the mother rejoiced in her strong, healthy boy! How I rejoiced in God Who had answered my call for help!

Classes went on as usual. As I left the classroom each day at noon and at the end of the day, I looked forward to being at home with George and the children; but many times, people were already waiting outside for me. I thanked God for allowing me, a simple farm girl, to be His servant to so many. I can testify that God was faithful to guide and help me because I could not otherwise have done the things I was asked to do. I often commented, "I feel constantly my need to depend on Him, especially when realizing I am not a doctor, only a registered health attendant for the area."

I was dumbfounded one day when a lady came to me saying that she could not hear but that she often heard a noise in her ears. I had heard of unusual items being found in the noses and ears of children, but I was astonished to find this adult woman's ears full of ticks. Some of them were very large while others were extremely small. I removed them one by one, fifteen ticks in all. This really shouldn't have been surprising since I had observed many animals in the homes that I visited, once seeing a chicken and a dog snuggled up on a bed with the family. Outside of most of the homes would be a pig or two, a few chickens, and always a dog. The pig and chickens were food for the family, but the dog was there to guard against thieves that might come during the night or when the family was away.

Once I was asked to deliver a baby in Pulquina Ariba, a small village about a mile upriver. This called for crossing the river, then hiking a trail to a small adobe house. I noticed that there were few windows which meant that there would be little light inside. Upon entering the dim room where the laboring woman lay, I hurriedly began to prepare for the birth. The woman's pains were coming quite often, and I knew it would not be long before the baby would arrive. Upon examination, I found that it would be necessary to break the water, and as I did so, I saw that the baby's head was crowning. After three more contractions, the baby was born. Silence filled the room. The baby had not cried. I picked him up by his feet and spanked his bottom. He still made no sound. I quickly covered the baby's mouth with gauze and performed mouth-to-mouth resuscitation. He still did not cry. Not a sound came from that little mouth. The father was watching and had moved to stand by a door. He stood silently, and then I saw him reach behind the door for a shovel.

"Here, I will take him and bury him," he stated sternly.

"No!" I cried out. Silently, I prayed, "Lord, help me. Show me what to do, Lord."

I asked for cold water. A woman rushed to get it, returning it with pleading eyes looking into mine. Seeking a miracle, she held out the glass. I took it from her and threw it on the infant. When the cold water touched the baby, he gasped, then released a most beautiful cry, a wonderful sound for all to hear. Realizing that his son lived, the father turned and replaced the shovel behind the door, saying, "Good, he is a worker." He knew that this boy would be a big help in the field, helping to provide food for the family table.

Other nurses who have heard of my experiences state that they would never touch some of the difficult cases I attended. I can understand their response since they are taught not to do anything without a doctor's approval. I saw myself as being under the direct instruction of the Great Physician, the Lord Jesus Christ. I served with a desire for others to see the Lord who was my strength and my shield (Psalm 28:7) and in total dependence on Him as my guide. He was always sufficient to lead me and to provide in every moment of need.

A missionary pastor who had lived in Bolivia for many years explained to George and me that one of the biggest problems he faced was helping the people understand that stealing and dishonesty were sin. Limited resources and opportunities often became the justification for wrong choices. The people were poor and had been taught that it is not wrong to steal in order to survive the challenges of life. Anyone who traveled anywhere must stay alert and guard their valuables from potential thieves who were quick and slick.

On one of my trips to deliver a baby before I had received my bicycle, I noticed a man gathering wood in the forest but continued on my way to the home where I had been called.

After delivering the baby and caring for the mother, I set out for home. As I started through the wooded area, I became very uneasy when I saw the man who had been gathering firewood earlier. I began to walk faster and tried to get around him, but he was faster. As I started to pass him, he grabbed me tightly. I struggled to free myself, but he was stronger and I could not get away from him. I cried out, "Lord, please help me. I am in a fix." As if in answer, the thought of my wedding ring came to me. I held up my hand for him to see. "Sir," I spoke in Spanish, "look at this. Look!" He saw it and released his grip, letting me go as if disgusted. I immediately ran on and rushed to the safety of my home and family. I was filled with thankfulness to God for giving me the thoughts and the words to help me, and I remembered that Jesus had said, "I will be with you always" (Matthew 28:19). "The Lord is my strength" (Psalm 28:7) was my experience repeatedly, and my faith grew stronger with each difficult situation I faced.

Once as I was walking home, a huge tarantula stood his ground on the path as if he would stop me. I accepted his challenge. I aimed as well as I could and stomped firmly on him. I apparently aimed well because he was squashed to nothing.

As I walked on and was about to cross the river to the mission station, a lady called out to me, "Come in and visit a minute, Señora." I recognized her as Maria who lived in a house along the trail. As I walked in to the clearing, I remembered the dream I had when I was only sixteen years old. I do not put much confidence in dreams, but this was special. There were so many details now being lived out that perfectly matched my dream. I saw this as extra confirmation that God had called me to missions even though I had never really had a doubt.

There was a log near the house, arranged for several people to sit and visit. Maria fanned the log before I sat down, as it was a common belief that sickness would result from sitting on a seat that is warm from the sun or from someone else sitting there. I sat on the log, surrounded by lush green trees, visiting and getting acquainted. Off to the side was a huge kettle from which I saw a duck, a pig, and some dogs and chickens eating their meal.

As I admired the surroundings, Maria offered me something to eat and I accepted. She went into her little kitchen and got a dish and a scoop and then went directly to the pets' big kettle. She dished up a scoop of its contents and brought it to me. As I glanced in the dish, I noticed the contents were moving: it was full of worms. George and I always agreed that we would eat whatever was offered to us because we did not want to offend anyone. I ate most of the "porridge" and left about a third of it on the dish. The custom was to eat all of something to indicate the desire for more. I did not think I wanted more. After visiting a while with Maria, I said goodbye and waded across the river toward home. Thankfully, I did not suffer any negative effects from my visit, and the experience so closely matching my dream filled me with the assurance that I was exactly where God wanted me to be.

Medical missionaries have often shared that doors of opportunity are opened to share the gospel when people are ill or near death, and I certainly found that to be true. The sick people I visited were usually more open to hearing of God's love for them and of His gift of eternal life. I believe that offering God's peace and comfort is an integral part of the healing process, and I delighted to testify of Him to these people in great physical need.

One day I was approached by a woman who appeared to be very weak and anxious. My face must have revealed my deep concern for her, because she instantly began to explain her disheveled appearance. On her journey to reach the mission, she had to cross a span of water. As she attempted to step out of the water onto the dry soil, her feet had slipped in the mud and she had fallen forward onto a half-buried large piece of glass.

Upon examining her wound, I discovered that the glass had pierced her stomach deep enough to reach her intestines but the intestines had not been cut. The wound was about two inches long, and I moved quickly to close it with stitches and to administer antibiotics. I was deeply concerned for she had traveled with an open wound exposed to the germs in the water, wearing wet, dirty clothes which clung to her body. This multiplied the chances of the intestinal area being exposed to contamination, thus increasing the possibility of severe infection. In the weeks following, her wound healed with no complications despite living far from any city where more professional help could have been found. I praised the Lord that the intestine was not perforated, because that could have led to a very different outcome.

On January 25, 1962, Robert Paul joined our family, and George was elated to have a son to carry on the Burt family name. Following the birth, we remained in Cochabamba for a few more days to allow the doctor to perform the circumcision on the eighth day. On that day, we arrived at the hospital dreading the procedure but understanding the benefits. We did not have to wait long before a nurse came and took Bobby into a room adjacent to our waiting room. Being so near Bobby proved comforting as well as heart-wrenching, for we were close enough to hear his cries. It was incredibly difficult for us to hear our baby's screams. At times he cried so hard that he struggled to breathe. With every cry, our own hearts cried out to God to hold Bobby in His protective hands. It seemed the doctor would never finish, but soon we received word that Bobby was fine. Fine! What a lovely word to hear at moments like this! Now my heart could better empathize with the parents who had brought their beloved little ones to me for care and then waited for their outcome.

Just two months later, Bobby and I found ourselves boarding another bus to make the long journey back to Cochabamba. Looking out the windows of the bus offered no real distraction and held little sunshine for my soul. My baby was gravely ill and I felt helpless. We finally reached the hospital where I once again placed my baby into the hands of others. Prior to leaving Tambo, radio contact had been made with personnel experienced in emergencies like the one we were facing. Bobby had a strangulated hernia which had occurred as a result of his severe crying during his circumcision. This situation had gradually worsened and was now critical. He could not keep down his milk, and there was blood when he spit up. Despite his serious condition, he did not receive immediate care when we arrived. Instead, we were sent to a doctor where I was given a list of supplies to be used for his surgery. I made the purchases, and Bobby and I returned to the hospital at six o'clock the following morning. Soon a nurse came, took Bobby and the supplies, and left me to wait and look to God. I was grateful that Bobby would be under anesthesia for this procedure and even more grateful to learn that the surgery had gone well. I was able to take Bobby home right away, and I returned, thankful that the operation had been performed in time to save his life.

That year at Christmas, Bobby received a large, red wooden truck. One of our special memories was that of our happy, healthy little boy gleefully playing with his truck, his first Christmas present. He loved it so much, and even as a grown man now, he treasures his memories of that delightful toy he played with as a little boy.

Following the Christmas vacation, as with all other holidays, the school's normal daily activities resumed, and I returned to my extremely busy routine of teaching and aiding people who needed medical attention. I often traveled to homes in the outlying villages, requiring a great deal of pedaling when I was already exhausted. I slowly began to realize that the stress and demand of my relentless schedule was taking a toll on my body. From time to time, I experienced a sharp, stabbing pain in my right abdominal area, but the severe pain would ease and I would continue my work. One day I was called to help someone who was sick in San Isidro. This would mean a long bike ride for me, and, to make matters worse, a strong wind always blew up in the afternoon. When I started back to the mission station, I found it very difficult to pedal against the strength of the wind. It was as if I took one step forward and then was blown two steps back. I nearly passed out from the effort, but I stopped and rested a few times and eventually arrived back at the mission station.

During our three-month summer vacation, George was away on a trip and Louise was sleeping in the bed with me when I began having severe pain. It was early morning, and Louise was afraid to go to the kitchen to get ice for me as it was still dark outside. In pain, I waited until it became lighter outside. I then sent her to the kitchen. After some time, the ice seemed to relieve the pain, but I knew I was dealing with symptoms and not the cause. Recognizing that I was in trouble, I had a staff member arrange by radio for the only bus of the day to pick me up on its way to Cochabamba. One of the other missionaries graciously agreed to take care of the children while I was gone. The bus I boarded was full of passengers, and even though I was obviously in severe pain, the bus driver directed me to sit on a bag in the aisle where I was very much aware of all the bumps in the road.

Thankfully, a doctor was available to examine me as soon as the bus arrived that night. I had already determined that I had appendicitis, so when I met with the doctor, I told him what my problem appeared to be. He performed his examination and confirmed that I would require an appendectomy. As was the practice, he gave me a list of supplies, and I endured a shopping trip for my own surgery even as I was experiencing severe abdominal pain. Early the next morning, I arrived at the hospital with the prescribed anesthesia, gauze, tape, stitching, and pain medication. Following the operation, the doctor told me that my appendix had been very inflamed and, at about twice its normal size, was about to burst. I had come just in time. George returned from his trip and after a couple of days of recovery, we returned to Tambo together.

Upon my arrival at Tambo, I was immediately met with urgent medical needs. Before we could even experience the satisfaction of being at home, I was informed by a staff member of a lady who had just arrived at the mission and wanted me to deliver her baby. I was extremely exhausted from my surgery and then the long, bumpy trip home, so I asked another missionary, my dear friend Anna Bailey, to assist me with the birth. After examining the mother, I informed her that she was carrying more than one baby. She was ordinarily a very small woman, but she was not small now, due to the babies she carried.

Whether because of added discomfort or custom, she chose not to lie down for the delivery, so I found a spike, drove it firmly into the top of the door casing, and then tied a small rope onto it for her to grasp while she squatted. This was a customary position used by the natives and a method many women preferred for an easier birth. Before long, the water broke and the first baby was born. I quickly tied and cut the umbilical cord. I then took time to instruct Anna to bathe and care for the baby while I delivered his twin. The first baby was not at all tiny, but the second baby was even larger, weighing close to ten pounds. Since we were still on our summer break, beds were available for the family to rest before traveling home.

Mother and both babies did very well, and the excited husband was able to take his new family home the next day.

Not all of my situations were positive. Some could only be described as heartbreaking. One such case was that of a young girl about twenty years old who walked from Pulquina Ariba to tell me about her problem. As I listened, I determined that she had a venereal disease. When I examined her, I was horrified by her condition. A portion of her body had been completely destroyed, the flesh consumed by this ravenous disease. I'll never know how she had the strength and endurance to make the long walk to Tambo in such unspeakable pain. She was beyond my help. I could offer her only medication to help ease her pain. She was extremely thin and frail; I judged from her condition that she would live no longer than three or four days.

As we talked, she admitted to a wayward lifestyle that had opened the door for this disease that she understood was now causing her death. I explained the gospel- how Jesus had died on the cross and had risen again to forgive her sin so that she could one day be with Him in heaven. She promised she would think about all that I had told her as she traveled with her parents to the place of her birth. Her family believed that a person should go back to the place of birth to die, so she would now endure excruciating pain as she journeyed on the back of a donkey across two rugged mountains to return to her birthplace. I heard later that she died four days after I saw her. I pray that she responded to the good news she heard before her death.

Once, a man from farther up in the mountains came to me with a large cut in his hand. He was extremely dirty, and it was obvious that it had been a long time since he had bathed or combed his hair. As I looked closer at his head, I could see worms moving through the strands of hair. As horrible as this may seem, it must be remembered that when there is only enough water for cooking and drinking, one has little time to worry about hair. During the cold season when there is little rain, there is little water for anything other than the most basic needs. After examining his hand, I determined he must have additional treatment with antibiotics. I gave him the pills, but he could not understand my dosing instructions. He was not accustomed to clocks and did not know how to read the time. Then I remembered what I had been told about some groups of people who could tell time by the sun. I began to give instructions again, this time describing the position of the sun at the times he was to take the medicine. This he understood and he went on his way back to his village, antibiotics in hand.

Another time, a man came on horseback, asking me to go with him to deliver a baby. He had thoughtfully brought a horse for me to ride, and we began our journey to "Two Pines," where we were to meet the laboring mother. As we arrived, I could look across another mountain and see the laboring mother being transported on an improvised stretcher. She soon arrived and was brought into the house and placed on the floor. I began to check her, and as I listened with the stethoscope, I was moved to sadness. I could hear no baby's heartbeat. I surmised the baby to be dead and began pushing the abdomen to deliver her stillborn baby. I did not know what had caused the problem, but the goal now was to help the mother rest and heal after her long ordeal. I was thankful that she recovered with no complications but sad that there had not been a more positive outcome.

There were many snakes in our area, and snake bite victims often came to me for medical help. A tourniquet of some sort had usually been applied to the area of the bite before I began my treatment. First, I administered a tranquilizer to help the person relax, then I gave antivenom for the particular kind of snake. Then I used my snake bite kit to draw out the venom. After a few minutes of rest, the pulse rate slowed down, and the patient was allowed to go home. They all seemed to get along fine after I attended them- for which I thank the Lord.

One moonlit night, George and I had a close call with a snake. We had walked across the road from the school to check on a neighbor who was suffering from malaria. After administering medication and visiting for a few minutes, we left to return home. Thankfully, we had not been requested to adhere to the custom among the people of the area: drink a glass of warm cow urine to cure and prevent malaria. This may be a case of the cure being worse than the disease! We knew that snakes often mate on moonlit nights, so we walked very carefully, watching our every step. George thought he had passed a twig, but I got a better look as I followed behind, and I cried out, "Kill that thing!" He immediately turned and aimed his flashlight in the direction of the twig and saw a good-sized yoperojabobo snake with his head lifted to strike. I had walked within three inches of that snake. We had been told that the bite of the yoperojabobo is deadly. Within minutes of being bitten, the victim becomes dizzy and often unconscious, with symptoms worsening rapidly leading to eventual death. We could not understand why the snake didn't strike, but we knew that God had protected us.

Sometimes people traveled from long distances and would need to find a place to stay near the mission while they were being treated. One such instance involved a two-year old boy who was dying. When the parents brought the child to me, he was too weak to cry and made only a faint whine. He was very dirty, and underneath the dirt, open sores covered his face and body. His tiny arms and legs were cold and bluish. He was so thin that there was no muscle mass in which to give an injection of antibiotic. His condition gave evidence to me that he had never sat up in his short life. I gently bathed him and tried again to give an antibiotic injection, this time successfully.

It was apparent that the mother had a mental illness that rendered her unable to understand how to feed and care for her son properly. Seeing the severity of the child's condition and the inability of the parents to care for him, I saw no opportunity for recovery. I made the decision to arrange for the child to remain with Señora Felicia who lived across the road from the school.

This dear lady owned goats, and she began to feed this dying child spoons of goat's milk throughout the day. After a time of observation, we decided to give him as much milk as he could comfortably consume. Señora Felicia was a marvelous caregiver who faithfully provided nourishing milk, soothing baths, and careful attention to his need of medication for the infected sores. Another missionary gave new clean clothes for him. Love was being shown to him by others, but his parents seemed more concerned about their animals back at home. I finally told them to go home and to return in three weeks for the child.

What a difference three weeks can make! When the parents returned, I sent word to Señora Felicia to bring the child to me. When she arrived with their little one, they refused to believe he was their child. They insisted that their son must have died. After I explained the care and treatment he had received, they were convinced that he was indeed the boy they had brought to me. They agreed to let him stay with us a little longer to continue his care. As proper daily care was given, the horrible sores healed. He gained weight. His muscles grew stronger, and he was now strong enough to roll himself over in his bed. He was eating soft foods now and was improving almost daily. Now he was able to sit up, and when the parents returned after the second three weeks, they truly struggled to believe that this was their child, alive and well!

I sat with the parents and explained very clearly how and when to feed the child. I stressed that if they were not careful, he would become ill again and possibly die. They took him home, leaving me with their promise that they would be diligent to feed him as instructed. I never saw them again, and I hoped that he continued to be healthy and strong.

Shortly after Louise's sixth birthday, we faced our own family emergency. Our girls slept in bunk beds with Rebecca in the lower bed and Louise in the top bunk. One morning before Louise climbed down from her high perch to get dressed, for some reason, she was sitting on the side of her bed with both arms tucked inside her pajama top. She lost her balance and fell forward and down onto the cement floor below. I ran to her and saw that her upper gum was cut open and her top four teeth were hanging in the gum but still attached. I carefully pushed the teeth and gum back into place, hoping that the teeth would reattach and that the gum would heal. Louise was on a liquid-only diet for several days and she was encouraged to try to hold her teeth together to help hold the gum in place.

We quickly decided that she must see a dentist, and Louise and I took the bus to Cochabamba. An examination revealed that the flesh was reattaching well, and she was to stay on liquids for a few more days. An X-ray showed that her permanent teeth had been pushed back up in the gum and might be late coming in. The dentist regretted to say that there was nothing he could do to help in this situation. When Louise's permanent teeth eventually emerged, they were not straight and she wore braces to correct them. She later had her wisdom teeth removed because her mouth was crowded. Those were the only ill effects she suffered from her fall.

After the dental examination, Louise and I boarded the bus to Tambo. After several hours, the driver announced that he was having trouble with the brakes. Unable to stop the bus, he began running the bus into the side of the mountain, trying to avoid careening over the edge and plunging all of us to serious injury or death. Finally, after several nerve-wracking minutes of banging and scraping, the driver was able to stop the bus. There were no houses in sight, and there were obviously no telephones here on this mountainside. The driver showed almost no emotion as he got off the bus and walked into the woods. We also got off, chattering nervously, wondering what would happen. The driver returned and announced that another bus was on the way and would take us on to Santa Cruz. We all knew that this was a lie. I did not know what the other passengers planned to do to reach their destinations, but I knew that Louise and I would not be safe in this place overnight. Asking for God's protection and help, I took Louise by the hand and stood with her beside our belongings at the roadside. I began to thumb for a ride, and the very first vehicle which came by stopped to pick us up. The driver recognized me and said that his destination was right beside the Tambo School. We were so thankful for God's obvious provision for our need.

Traveling in the mountains was always risky. There was the ever-present possibility of going over the edge of one of the cliffs. The road was narrow with no room for another vehicle to pass even if necessary, although there were a few designated places along the road that had been widened for the purpose of passing. The vehicle coming up the mountain had the right of way, and the vehicle going down must wait for it to pass. A driver's impatience often resulted in tragedy. One Sunday afternoon, I had just lain down to rest when someone came to tell me that there had been an accident and that three injured men had been brought to the school for medical treatment. A truck had fallen over the side of the mountain and the survivors had been pulled from the wreckage and placed on the grass in our patio area. I immediately joined the other staff members who had already gathered to help. It was apparent to all of us that all three men were in grave condition. My hasty examination revealed that one man had internal injuries, another was unconscious and the third had a serious head injury. I tended the wound as best as I could. We helped them as much as we could and then one of our men quickly transported them to the hospital in Santa Cruz. We later received news of the death of two of the three. All who were at Tambo were saddened but not surprised by this news.

Six years flew by quickly with more work than we could ever have imagined but also with many valuable lessons of God's faithfulness. George and I agreed that it was time for a furlough. Prior to leaving, we prayed for guidance from the Lord concerning where to serve for the next term. We then waited for His direction and were soon confident that we had fulfilled our purpose at Tambo and would move to a different but similar area for our second term. When the people near Tambo heard that our family would be leaving, they went to the authorities of the small town and attempted to arrange for the government to keep us from leaving! Of course, there were no legal grounds for us to be held, and so, when the school year ended, the Burt family packed up our belongings and began our journey to a time of rest in England. We traveled by plane from Tambo to Santa Cruz and then on to Argentina to visit with our friend, Dr. James Black and his wife Lola. After a few days of fellowship with these dear godly friends, the Burt family of five boarded a ship for England. We were on our way home.

*Ruthie and George with
14-month-old Louise
on the mission field in
Bolivia (chapter 3)*

*Esse-Ejja, a nomadic people group
in Bolivia (chapter 5)*

*George preaching in San
Buenaventura (chapter 5)*

*Burt family of seven (chapter 5) Louise,
Gilbert and Simon (raised as sons),
George, Rebecca, Bobby and Ruthie*

Bobby with a catch of flesh-eating pirañas

Village authorities approved Ruthie to start a medical post in Tushmo, Peru. (chapter 6)

A typical house in San Buenaventura, Bolivia

Timmy, one of the babies Ruthie helped deliver in Peru, was born with a deformed hip and leg but grew into a healthy adult after having surgery in the USA. (chapter 7)

Pastor Moises: George and Ruthie led him to the Lord as a 12-year-old boy. He now pastors a church in the Andes Mountains. (chapter 6)

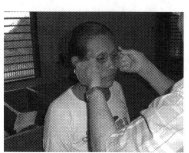

Fitting of 600 donated pairs of eyeglasses in Tushmo, Peru (chapter 7)

Preacher boy! Miguel Gonzales was very sick, and Ruthie nursed him back to health. Here he is preaching the dedication of his home church in San Lorenzo. (chapter 7)

Speaking at a ladies' prison Six were saved that day, one of whom had killed her husband and children. (chapter 7)

The church at San Lorenzo met in a small building that had been damaged by termites and then by a strong wind. The remaining pieces had been put back up with extra supports added. (chapter 7)

A new building for the Maranatha Baptist Church of Tushmo (chapter 7)

The Payunge Church, a church in Chile where God did a miracle! (chapter 7)

CHAPTER FIVE

STRENGTHENED

"…strengthened with all power, according
to His glorious might…"
Colossians 1:11

After a week on the ocean liner, we docked at South Hampton and rejoiced to see Mr. Good, the retired London police officer who had led George to the Lord. We were excited but exhausted, and Mr. Good had thoughtfully arranged for us to be taken to a Christian camp where we would have a week of relaxation. After that week, he provided an apartment for us where we stayed until the finish of our stay in England. Arrangements were also made for us to present our mission work in local churches. During the first half of our furlough, George and I attended meetings where we shared about our work in Tambo and then presented our plans for work to be done in the Beni area. No support resulted from these meetings, and we were told later that missionaries not already affiliated with the church at which they spoke would not receive support. We were not concerned by this but considered it to be part of God's plan. We were always pleased to share with others about the Lord's work, and this led to our prayer that our sharing be used to put a burden for missions on the hearts of those who heard our message.

Spending time with George's relatives and friends was the primary goal for our time in England. One sunny, blue-sky day, the family visited a friend who took us to her backyard to see her flowers. As we were all admiring the beautiful beds of plants, she noticed some weeds and bent over to pull them. Four-year-old Rebecca, quite observant and very outspoken, was following directly behind the somewhat heavyset lady and had been making her own observations. She proclaimed loudly, "My, you have a big bottom on you, don't you?" Politely, the gracious lady continued without responding to the childish remark. After walking about in the lovely garden of lavender, pink and yellow irises, and roses, we went back inside where the lady told her sister what Rebecca had said to her in the garden. Rebecca overheard the conversation, and everyone in the room heard her chime in without a moment's hesitation: "Well, you do have a big bottom, don't you?" Everyone burst into laughter, and we have a lasting memory of our gracious hostess and our outspoken daughter.

We also visited Stonehenge since it was not far from where we were staying, and that interesting excursion left many questions in our minds. How in the world did the ancient people move those huge stones, and how did they place them on top of other stones? We enjoyed all our activities but especially the time spent with dear people.

Now it was time for the second half of our year-long furlough, six months in the United States. We arrived at the American Embassy in London to get visas for George and Louise, then for Rebecca and Bobby who had been born in Bolivia. We were delighted by how quickly the visas were granted. The officials then asked to check my papers. When they returned, they came with a shock we had not expected: they informed me that I was no longer a citizen of the United States of America. I could not believe my ears. I had always thought I had dual citizenship. As I stood, still in shock, I was given a form and asked to sign it. The form was titled "Loss of Citizenship," and I responded, "I do not want to sign the form." The official's response was not encouraging. I was told that I would not be granted a visa to enter the United States unless I signed the form. Blinking to hold back tears, I reluctantly signed the form and was granted a visa, but I vowed at that moment that I would do everything I could to regain my American citizenship.

We were now ready to make the flight from London to our home for the next six months: the wonderful USA. At this time, the Concord had just started making flights to America, and we had the pleasure of flying on the Concord to New York City. We traveled by a smaller plane to Erie, Pennsylvania, where we were welcomed by my parents and Dr. Augustine, the pastor of my home church in East Springfield. What a thrill to be with these dear people!

We were blessed to be able to live in a house just a block away from my parents' home. When George and I had speaking engagements, Grandma and Grandpa stayed with our children and were a blessing to all of us. The speaking engagements were a very important part of our preparation for future service because the churches where we spoke often became our supporters. When we left seven years earlier, we were promised $150 in monthly support. This was not enough for a family of three, but God had stretched those dollars and was always faithful to provide for our needs, even when we became a family of five. We made new friends and renewed former friendships.

Once again, my home church took care of the passage expense for us to return to the field. George and I were so thankful for a pastor and congregation who cared so much about missions and who encouraged us in every way they could. We praised God Who supplied our every need and stretched the small to make it more than enough.

The time passed quickly, and the difficult moment of parting arrived. It was time to travel to Cochabamba, Bolivia, once again. Bolivia consists of nine main subdivisions, known as departments. This time, we were on our way to the Beni Department, a hot jungle area. It would be a great change from the Andes Mountains, in climate and in surroundings, and, as we would soon find out, in the way the people lived.

Our family of five enjoyed an exhilarating flight from Cochabamba to La Paz and then from La Paz to the village of Rurrenabaque. The pilot skillfully maneuvered the two-motor plane down through the mountain corridor, dropping so low that it seemed we would clip the trees with the wings of the plane. As we made our way down to the lowlands, temperatures were warmer and plant life was in abundance. Soon we were right at the base of the mountains and as far as we could see, everything was flat. Our plane came in for a landing on a small grass runway. Waiting near the air strip was an old flatbed truck that transferred passengers and their baggage to Rurrenabaque. From there, we traveled by canoe across the Beni River to San Buenaventura, the village where we would be stationed. The canoe trip provided a breathtakingly beautiful view of green tropical plant life. We were now in tropical surroundings and were very much aware of the tropical heat.

The villagers' homes were made of bamboo sticks secured with vines. The roofing was usually palm leaves. Here among the palms, lizards and insects could often be heard scurrying around. A smaller building behind each home provided kitchen space. The homes and the kitchens had mud floors. We moved into a house that had belonged to a missionary couple who had previously worked in the village. The husband had been appointed to administrative duties, requiring them to move to Cochabamba.

The day after we arrived in the village, Rebecca became very ill. She did not eat for three days, and we were very concerned. On the fourth day, we woke to find that she was not in her bed. Where could she be? We started searching immediately and were relieved to find her sitting in one of the lower kitchen cabinets, happily eating bananas- a good sign that she was recovering from her sickness!

The previous missionary couple had started a church which met in the large living room of the home. A church building with a thatched roof with a large overhang was later built on an adjoining lot. A small ditch formed around the house with the dirt against the building causing a nice drain-off when it rained. The building was adobe brick with two or three windows on each side. The windows had no glass but consisted of hard, wooden bars about four inches apart to provide security. The open windows allowed a comforting breeze to pass through the building. In the Amazon Basin tropical jungle, a breeze of any size was greatly valued by all, especially those who were inside a building for any length of time.

Our goal after getting settled was to get acquainted with the people and to begin to communicate our desire to help them. We wanted to encourage the believers and to share the gospel with those who either had not heard or had not yet believed. The people here were mainly of the Tacana group, but there were some from other groups from areas farther down the river. The Tacana people now spoke Spanish as their main language, although the older members of the group could still speak their native Tacana language. As they grew to realize our willingness to help them, they began to come to our home when they had a medical need. Gradually, the doors of their homes opened to me, especially when a woman was in labor and needed assistance with the birth. The Lord had allowed me to develop many medical skills during my stay in Tambo, and we were thankful to see Him use them to draw people to Himself here as well.

During our first few weeks, many kind villagers brought us fruit. This was a blessing, but the kitchen had to be stocked with other food as well. It was possible to buy some things in Rurrenabaque: groceries, kerosene, and material for making clothing. With the use of a two-way radio which was in the house when we arrived, we were able to contact the mission buyer in Cochabamba for a shipment of fresh vegetables to be sent by plane a few times during the year. Our main staples were rice, bananas, and yucca. If we had meat, it was whatever meat the people offered to sell us. Fish, wild pig, monkey, tapir, turtle, and whatever else was found in the jungle often filled the kerosene refrigerator in our kitchen. This refrigerator served to cool water and keep food from spoiling. We could also purchase avocados, oranges, mangos and a variety of other fruits from the people, providing us with quite a variety of food.

For clean drinking water, we had brought with us a ceramic water filter. A fifty-five-gallon barrel located at the eaves on the back side of the house caught rainwater. One day we noticed that a horse had become interested in our rain barrel. When the horse wanted water, it would take the clothespins off the edge of the barrel to free the cloth covering which kept the water clean. Then take hold of the cloth, pull it off and have a drink. It was such fun to watch her sneak that drink!

I had to make my own bread for the family, so I rose early in the morning to prepare the dough. Without fail, when I was in the middle of mixing the dough, someone would come to the door. I must put aside my dough and wash my hands to go to the door. I invited my guest inside and offered them a seat. They sat silently for a while until at last, they decided to talk and tell me why they had come. After taking care of the need, the visitor would leave and I would return to the dough. While I was still working with the dough, another visitor would arrive. Some mornings the same procedure of visitation would take place three or four times before I was able to knead the dough and let it set to rise. With each disruption of my morning, I attempted to meet the needs patiently, but I began to let the interruptions bother me and bread-making became a very frustrating ordeal. Then the Lord began to do a work in my soul, creating in me a question: "Ruthie, why are you here?" I asked myself, and it did not take long before the answer was evident. It really did not matter what time of day the bread was prepared. God had not sent us here to be bakers of bread but to be fishers of men. These people were far more important than my bread. These were people to whom God had sent me to share the gospel and His love. Instead of seeing this as a trial, I began to see it as an opportunity. It was now easier to see the interruptions as calls for help and to be thankful that God was allowing me to share Him as the Source of help. He was helping me as well. In my weakness, He heard my cry for help and He was my strength. With His help, my attitude of frustrated bread-making became an attitude of loving service.

We gradually settled into our new surroundings, and our children learned to be a part of village life. It was not unusual to see animals grazing freely in the village because most of the natives allowed their pigs and other animals to run free. The inevitable happened one afternoon when our adventurous Rebecca was outside playing. I heard a pig squealing and looked out to discover the cause of all the commotion. There to my amazement was our little Rebecca straddling a pig, holding on for dear life, tightly gripping the pig's skin and hair. With her little fingers intertwined in what little hair there was, she rode that pig for about two hundred feet. The neighbors were watching the performance and seemed to enjoy every moment. It was as if we had our own little pig rodeo.

Life was not always easy for us or for the children. There were dangers to be faced, and our children learned to recognize God's hand of protection and help. One day Rebecca and I went to the river to play. We had been there only a short while when I heard a ping on the stones in the riverbank behind me. Someone from the nearby island was shooting at me! I hurriedly told Rebecca that we needed to go to the house, but before she could get out of the water, another shot rang out, again missing its target. A third shot also missed, perhaps because I kept us moving around, but perhaps even more because the Lord was our protection and our shield (Psalm 18:2).

After putting the children to bed one night, George and I settled down in the living room which was next to the children's bedroom. We were just enjoying time talking together when we heard whimpering. I got up to check on the children and discovered that the mosquito netting had been chewed and Rebecca's finger was bleeding. We surmised that she must have had her hand against the mosquito netting when a rat attacked. We had heard scuffling at night and had guessed that the noises were made by rats. Now we felt sure of it. When we tried to deter them by aiming a flashlight in the direction of their noises, we could hear several rats scamper away. How I would have liked to have one of the big, fat barn cats from back home! One day while in the kitchen, I saw a rat's tail sticking out from behind something. Quietly reaching for a butcher knife, I cut off the tail. The rat scampered away, but two days later, we saw it outside near the house. We eventually eliminated most of them by setting poison out at night and then removing it the following morning.

Rats became such a problem in our area that in the village of San Jose they caused the deaths of five people in one family and two in another. A commission came through the villages to investigate and to set poison out for the rats. They discovered that rats were getting into the store at night and were urinating on the rice that was stored in burlap bags. Many of the people took tri-sulfa pills, and there were no other rat-related deaths. The plague had not yet spread to other villages and now they had learned how to keep it from spreading if there should be a breakout in the future. Sometime later, an article about this plague was published in *Reader's Digest*.

There were other pests in the area as well. Army ants were fearless and capable of great damage to anything they could digest. We once saw a long line of army ants moving along our fence, then on the grass, making their way to our house. It looked as if they were soldiers out to destroy anything in their path. Thankfully, we saw them in time to hurry for buckets full of a substance they do not like: water. After being drenched, they scattered, and we were thankful we did not have to deal with them en masse. Another day, I had just gotten situated in the outhouse when I noticed that I had inadvertently stirred up a big cluster of ants which were now moving rapidly toward me. I vacated my private quarters quickly before they swarmed me. I returned with my weapons of destruction and two buckets of H_2O got rid of the ants for the time being. Bobby, too, had a close call in the outhouse. He had just gotten settled and when he looked around, he saw a big snake curled up in the corner. He got up quickly but moved slowly to avoid catching the snake's attention and got out safely. It was necessary to be on the lookout for ants and snakes at all times.

Louise attended school at Tambo, requiring a flight to Cochabamba via La Paz before the start of a new school year. I went with her to get her settled in and to help her start the term feeling confident and secure. Louise was very interested in our fellow passengers. Turbulence caused our plane to lunge up and down, and a gentleman seated in front of us began to be in obvious discomfort. The violent lunging was causing him excruciating pain, and Louise was very concerned for him. Then, there was another lunge, and he became totally still. Death had claimed this man who had suffered from a strangulated hernia and had been on his way to La Paz to have surgery. Louise wanted to know what had happened to him. I knew it was important to explain truthfully but carefully so as not to frighten her. I offered her an explanation she could understand and then changed the topic of conversation so that she would not dwell on what had happened. As the flight continued, I observed that she seemed to have processed what had happened without being upset by it and I was thankful for that.

That year, George and I were able to teach in the village public schools. Religion was taught in Bolivian schools then, and Roman Catholic teachers had been invited to teach but had not accepted the invitation. This opened the door for our ministry, and we taught God's Word to public school students, providing many opportunities to teach about the life of Christ. We taught only one year because the trips we had to make by river and by trail to reach the villages took us away from our own place of service.

George and I made a river trip to visit a couple who had trusted Christ as Savior several years earlier when the previous missionary had been there. On our way, the boat had to be directed carefully between large boulders that were almost impossible to see as they were just beneath the surface of the river. Despite the efforts of the men who guided the boat, we missed the pass and hit the boulders. We were stuck. The men tried to free the boat, but we were taking on water and something must be done. They managed to unload the cargo and leave it at a house along the riverside. We moved on downriver while some of the men continued scooping out water. We arrived safely at our destination and enjoyed two days of fellowship with the couple, spending time reading and discussing the scriptures with them. We returned home, taking the same boat, not fully repaired but sufficient to take us back home.

George was a faithful witness, and many people heard the gospel through him as we made our way to the villages. God was always faithful to lead and protect, and this became obvious to us one day when George made plans to travel to Tumupasa and Ixiamas. He planned his day of departure, but his plans were changed at the last minute. We later learned that the leader of a church across the river had made this same trip two weeks before George had planned to go. Word reached us that a woman had been given poison to put in bread for George to eat when he arrived. She did make the bread and she did indeed add the poison, but her intended victim did not come. When he finally went a few weeks later, the poison had already been used and George was safe.

We experienced a very troubling incident in the village one night. One of our neighbors at the front along the riverside, Tirina, had hosted a drinking party at his house that evening. A fight had broken out which resulted in Tirina getting his pistol and shooting one of his guests in the leg. Now this guest was a military officer from the army base located across the river on the outskirts of Rurrenabaque. Someone left the party and went across the river to the military base to report that Tirina had shot the officer. In what seemed only minutes, several military personnel came for Tirina. For our protection, George had turned all of our lights off, but we could still see and hear what was happening. The soldiers led Tirina around our lot, one on either side holding a gun to his head. His young children followed, crying and begging the soldiers not to shoot their father. As they marched him around the third side of our house, they shot him. There had been no trial, no representation.

Seeing a man killed so needlessly and with no remorse was a stark picture of the evil of unregenerate man. Our hearts grieved for those who walked in such darkness (1 John 2:11).

Meanwhile, back at Tambo, the school year ended with a delightful surprise. Louise had done so well in school that the director suggested the possibility of her skipping the fifth grade. We were very proud of her diligence. The children always performed plays at the end of each school year, and this year, there was a girl who just would not learn her lines. As the time for the performance began to draw near, the girl's part was given to Louise who had already learned all the lines. Of course, George and I were the proud beaming parents at that play. After summer vacation, Louise entered the sixth grade and proved herself equal to the task. She was always attentive and quick to learn new things.

It came to our attention that there was a man downriver who was skilled in building boats. The man had escaped from Germany near the end of World War II. It was rumored that he had served Hitler and had been involved in the inhumane deaths of thousands of Jews. We knew that many who had committed war crimes had avoided execution by going to South America, and we were not sure how God wanted us to respond to this man. We needed a boat, but we did not know if we should do business with him. We sought God's guidance and later went to him to ask him to build a boat for the outboard motor we had brought with us. He did make the boat which we named the Florecita. We often made short trips along the river, stopping at any villages where we were permitted to share the Word.

On one of our river trips, George and I made contact with some of the Esse-Ejja people. They loved tapitapi, (sugar) which we happened to have with us and which we traded with them for meat. After this trade which pleased them greatly, we stayed to visit with the people. One family had a pet monkey which entertained the children and delighted us as well. To our great surprise, the monkey suddenly left the children and moved toward the children's mother. Climbing up on her, it proceeded to nurse, and the mother did not respond negatively. A few minutes later, the woman's baby started fussing and she allowed the little one to nurse without any cleansing following the monkey's nursing. In this culture, nothing was known of germs or sanitation. Interestingly, we learned that people in these settings build up their own immunities that benefit and protect them.

We spent the rest of the afternoon enjoying the beach and walking on the jungle trails. Deciding this would be a good place to stay for the night, we cut bamboo for uprights and spread the top with bamboo leaves, thus providing protection from mosquitoes and from rain. After setting up our sleeping area, we ate a simple meal and then climbed under the mosquito netting for some rest. Sleeping on the *playa* (beach) was a pleasant experience that night. The playa was sandy and provided a comfortable rest area for our family.

As a safety measure, George and I always placed our very active little Bobby between us to sleep. How thankful we were that we did so this night! From a sound sleep, we woke to the sound of a tiger sniffing around our mosquito netting. We lay perfectly still as if frozen, almost afraid to breathe. "Please Lord, don't let Bobby wake from his sound sleep," I prayed, knowing that the least little noise might result in a tragic outcome. After waiting, waiting for what seemed hours yet was in reality only a few minutes, the tiger turned and walked away, leaving us to praise God for His protection and mercy. We were told by the nationals that the tigers did not usually bother people in the nets, and we thanked the Lord for His provision of the netting and the safe place to sleep that night.

Since I worked with the Ministry of Health in La Paz on

inoculation programs for childhood diseases, I arranged for the Esse-Ejja mothers to bring their children to our house for their shots. On the designated day, we woke early to the sounds of chatter outside. They had all come: the children and their mothers and fathers. We sprang into action quickly and began to organize the people. The children's names and their ages had to be listed on the health report, but when we asked for that information, it was not unusual for a child to answer, "Yesterday I was Bill, but I don't want to be him anymore." I eventually gave them names and asked them not to change them, but I don't know if those names stuck with them or not. The children received shots three times with six weeks in between inoculations. Although I noticed that there were slightly fewer children each time, I enjoyed the program very much, believing it to be of great help in the children's health. One little boy was so terrified of receiving a shot that it took three women to hold him. As I drew near with the needle, he grabbed the syringe like lightening and threw it. It stuck in the wall like a dart, and I was thankful that it had not hit anyone in that room full of people milling about. As I continued with the job of administering the shot, I looked behind me just in time to see an elderly grandmother fall to the floor with her legs crossed beneath her just as they had been when she was sitting on the seat we had provided for our guests. Now two ladies were sitting there! I got the impression none of them had ever sat on a padded seat before! So the two ladies unseated with a push the grandmother so they could have a try at such a special treat.

In the Amazon Basin, it often rains extremely hard with a great deal of rain falling in a short period of time. One afternoon, a strong heavy rain had resulted in about six inches of water standing everywhere, even under our house which had been wisely built on stilts. We had been waiting impatiently for the rain to end, and now the sun was beaming. I grabbed my rubber boots, hurriedly pulling them on as I went outside to check on everything. I was enjoying a quiet stroll, breathing in the smell of the fresh air after the rain, when, suddenly, a bolt of lightning struck the wet ground right in front of me. My neighbor screamed, thinking I had been struck. As the bolt hit, it spread out over the water in all directions, but I was not harmed. Both my neighbor and I thought for some time to come about that amazing display of God's protection.

We learned more about the people as we traveled up and down the river, village to village. We talked about how we would feel if strangers came to our home and told us about a God we had never known. If we had never heard the good news of Jesus, how strange it would sound! We asked ourselves, would we be so ready to accept what they were telling? The Lord impressed on us that it would take great patience, a tremendous amount of prayer, and trust in the Holy Spirit to build relationships with the people with whom we wanted to share the gospel. We began by attempting to get better acquainted with them, building friendships and showing them God's love, trusting Him to open their souls to His word when it was presented.

Gilberto was one of the special individuals the Lord brought into our lives. Before we met him, his father had died from tuberculosis and he had apparently contracted it from his dad. The government had selected a few villages in the jungle area in which to establish small clinics which they referred to as hospitals, and in one of these, Gilberto lay at the point of death. The young child was in a coma and the staff could not find a pulse.

His mother, Tina, was desperate. She walked out behind the hospital, alone, crying out in agony to her son's God. Gilberto had trusted Christ as his Savior, but Tina had not yet believed. Now she pleaded for the life of her child. She didn't truly know how to pray because she did not yet know God, so she tried to make a bargain with Him. If God would keep her son alive, she would accept Him as her God. After a short while, she returned to Gilberto's room. She touched his neck, feeling for a sign of life. Was the God her son loved so much mighty enough to save her little boy? Her trembling fingers brought to her a message: there was a pulse. Joyfully, she called for the nurse who confirmed Gilberto's pulse; he was alive!

The nurse explained to Tina that the hospital administration had already asked for a Catholic priest to come to administer last rites. While she had been outside pleading with God, the priest had come and placed a wafer in Gilberto's mouth. Now the boy was coming out of the coma, and as those around him started to explain all that had occurred, including the wafer still in his mouth, he spit it out and proclaimed, "I am still a Christian!"

A few years later when Gilberto was only twelve years old, the aunt and uncle with whom he had been living told him he would need to find a new place to live. When we heard about this, we began to pray for God's guidance. We knew of his illness and desired to help him. We felt a peace about him coming to live with our family and trusted that God could protect us from the tuberculosis he carried in his body. We were happy to add Gilberto to the Burt family.

Gilberto had been with us several months when the story of another young boy touched our hearts. Saul was also twelve and was a friend of Gilberto's. Saul told us that he and his siblings had been horribly mistreated in their home. His mother had killed one of his sisters by pushing her to the floor and stomping on her throat. Later, another of the children was killed in the same manner. Now we learned that the brutal mother had arranged to sell her son into slavery. She had met a man who made his living by enslaving other men whom he sent into the jungle to harvest nuts, jerky, and other items he could sell. These men were forced to survive on whatever food they could find in the jungle, and sickness and disease often claimed their lives. There was little hope of ever coming out alive.

This woman had decided to send her twelve-year-old child into this just for him to have a pair of pants. This woman had decided the pants would convince him to go. There was only one course of action for the Burts. We asked him to come to live with our family. Without hesitation, he answered with a resounding, "Yes!"

We were a family of seven now, and saving money was a must. My days were often occupied with sewing, making shirts for the boys and dresses for the girls and myself. Housework and medical visits from our new friends filled my days, but I delighted in our household of children. Louise loved to read and to study. Gilberto was quiet and studious, preferring to do homework rather than spend time with other kids his age. Simon was a bit mischievous and did not spend as much time with his studies, thus having to be corrected more often. Rebecca was content to entertain herself and was often in her own little world. Bobby was playful and happy with his four older siblings.

All the children loved the river, and they swam every day that the water was not muddy or too high. When the river was high, it was interesting to watch huge trees being swept downstream and carried away as if they were only matches. One never knew what those rapidly moving waters would bring our way. Once, a suitcase with an unusual passenger came on the high rushing water. A very frantic chicken was running back and forth, side to side, trying to keep its balance on that suitcase.

Bobby was quite good at carving, and with the help of Gilberto, carved canoes and boats to carry to the river when he went swimming. He also made a little bow and arrow. One day he was practicing with his bow and had placed a small object on the ground to use as a target. Stepping away from the target, he drew the arrow back, took careful aim, and released the arrow.

He was surprised to see one of our chickens running across the yard into the path of the arrow. Bobby was distraught! We caught the chicken and removed the arrow and reassured Bobby that we understood that it was an accident. Bobby's tears subsided when he realized that the arrow shooting was not fatal and the chicken would survive the ordeal.

June, July and August provided a nice vacation for the children, but it soon came to an end. Bobby was now old enough to join Louise when she returned to school. George and I once again planned a trip to visit the people in the village of Tumupasa, a two-day jaunt on the trails, and Gilberto and Saul would go with us. We took along some sandwiches which took care of our midday hunger pains. Our only problem was the hundreds of mosquitoes who were also hungry. We were in constant battle, swatting at the multitude of insects attacking us. We ate our simple lunch and resumed our hike down the trail to where we would spend the night. We arrived at a designated place for travelers to lodge and receive food. We put our mosquito netting in place and crawled in, expecting a sound sleep after the day's walking. We felt a fine spray coming through the net, settling on our faces. Thinking we might be mistaken, we wiped our faces to remove the moisture and once again we felt it on our faces and arms. Even with this continuing to occur, we were so tired that we soon fell into a deep sleep.

The next morning, we were up and ready for another full day of walking the trail. We asked our hosts about the wet spray we had felt after getting in the mosquito nets. The lady of the house informed us that the moisture was simply bats urinating as they flew overhead, a normal occurrence after dark. Needless to say, a good scrubbing was in order! We were served breakfast, and then we were on our way.

Once again, mosquitoes were our travel companions. They were so thick in the woods that we must fan constantly to avoid being bitten, but there were pleasant sights to behold as well. Beautiful, colorful parrots and tropical fauna and flora kept us busy looking in all directions. It was late afternoon as we neared the village of Tumupasa to meet another group of Tacana friends. I was excited as we entered the village, anticipating being with the people. I was drawn to a woman who was sitting on a very low stool with a large loom in front of her. She was weaving something that looked like it might be used on a bed. I was so intent on watching her work that I was not watching where I was walking. I came to a sudden stop with my face right against the back end of a horse. I heard laughter from the villagers and I was embarrassed, but my goof had given the people a laugh, and more importantly, it had broken the ice for conversation.

We walked about three hundred feet more to reach the house where we would stay that night. The lady of the house made us feel very welcomed. She served us a delicious meal and visited with us for a long while, then showed us where we would be sleeping: the mud floor. She went out and soon came back with a palm leaf mat to lay on the floor. After crawling in under the mosquito netting and tucking the edges under all around the mat, we were ready to sleep. We soon became aware that the mat made a good place for roaches to hide because we felt them crawling on us during the night.

The next day, we were given permission to host a meeting in the school. The school was filled with villagers who came out of curiosity to see the visitors. We showed slides about Christ and His life and George narrated, explaining the gospel in words they could understand. We don't know that anyone made a response to the message that night, but we were told that it was their first opportunity to hear the gospel.

The next two days were spent traveling back home to San Buenaventura. After we had been home a few days, someone told me that the Señora Pinto was on her death bed and I knew I must go to visit her. She lived just over an hour's walk going down the trail toward Tumupasa. I asked Gilberto's sister Chela to go with me and we prepared our things including mosquito nets as we would probably stay overnight. I was told that the priest did not want to go because it had rained so much and the trail was very muddy. When we reached what was usually only a small stream of water, it was now a roaring creek. We realized that we should not try to cross it until someone else came along. Then we could manage if three secured our arms together. Finally, a man came, and the three of us started across, with our packs high up on our shoulders and our arms linked tightly together. We struggled and made it across in spite of large stones hitting our legs.

When we arrived at Señora Pinto's home, it was starting to get dark and her two sons reluctantly showed us to her bedside. I said to her, "Señora, do you realize you are going to leave this world?"

She was very weak and could barely speak. In a faint voice, she answered, "Yes."

Then I told her the story of Jesus' love and how He loved her enough to give His life for her. I explained more as she lay there listening. We soon left her to rest and think about what we had talked about, and we looked for a place to spend the night. We found our way to the back and saw a lean-to where we could put up our mosquito nets and hunker down for the night.

It started raining again, and even though we were able to stay dry, we would not get much sleep if there was any wind. Chela was resting against a pile of corn waiting to be taken off the cob, and I was on the outside. The family's large pig decided to lie down right against me! There he was, grunting, moving around trying to get comfortable, and rubbing his mud all over my back. The rain continued all night, and we didn't get much sleep. In the morning, we found that by standing under the eaves we could allow the rain to wash away the mud we had acquired from our unusual bedfellow!

We packed up the mosquito nets and were ready to see Señora Pinto. As she rested, I invited her to put her trust in Jesus and be forgiven of her sins. She listened intently and soon began to pray in a very weak voice, asking the Lord Jesus to forgive her and to be her Savior. After she prayed, we spent a few minutes encouraging her and then we turned back to the muddy trail toward home. Some might wonder, was it worth all the rain and mud and sleeping with a pig, and I answer, "Yes! I would do it again to see someone give their heart to the Lord."

The men often went alligator hunting near the end of the rainy season, just as the water started to go down. The women went along to cook and to salt the meat to preserve it until they returned to the village to sell it. A trip typically lasted about three weeks or even longer. Two excited couples began their hunting trip early one morning and were getting into their canoes when one of the women, Cleautilde, stepped on a nail in a piece of wood that was caught in the mud. She thought nothing of it and assured everyone that she would be fine. They continued their hunt over the next two or three weeks and actually captured and killed some of those evasive animals.

Even before they started down the river heading home, Cleautilde's heel and her leg all the way up to her knee had become red, hot, and swollen- double the size of her other leg. She was in a great deal of pain by the time they reached home. Her husband took her to a small government clinic to have her leg examined. The doctor there told him that her leg needed to be amputated at once in order to save her life. As if that were not bad enough, he told them that the clinic had no anesthesia available. Her husband responded firmly, "No!" He left Cleautilde in their care and travelled for days through the jungle until he found another small clinic. There the doctor told him that there was no anesthesia. The discouraged husband made his way back to the clinic where his wife was suffering.

He took his wife home from the clinic and immediately came to me. Now everyone passed the word along that she would die because he would not consent to the amputation. When he reached my home, he explained his wife's condition to me and asked me to come to examine her. Seeing his desperation, I agreed to go. Upon arrival, I found what seemed to be the entire village gathered outside their home. As I approached the house, everyone shushed, waiting to see what would happen next. They all waited quietly to hear what I would say.

I found the woman in excruciating pain and hurried to examine her wound. As I unwrapped the leg, a stench filled the room and even passed through the spaces of the bamboo walls so that the people began to move away from the house. It was difficult for me to stay, too, but I wanted to be faithful to this woman who needed help. I told her husband that I did not know what was possible but that I would ask for God's help to not only save her life but also restore her leg. I made one request: if he wanted me to attend her, he would have to forget the witch doctor. If he wanted the witch doctor, he would have to forget me. He made his choice: "I want you."

Before I did anything else, I went home and consulted the medical books that my nurse friend had given me years earlier. Then I went back to her house and asked for a bucket of warm water. After having Cleautilde soak her leg in the water, I applied gentle pressure which caused the leg to open. Pus exploded from the leg in various places, but Cleautilde made no reaction. I continued this pressure once a day for about three days. I administered the needed units of penicillin daily. I trimmed away all the bad flesh first right down to tendon and bone. Then I covered the incision with sterilized Brazil nut oil.

On the tenth day of treatment, I noticed small pink spots appearing in her heel, and Cleautilde's hope was renewed when I told her that this was new flesh beginning to grow. It wasn't long until she could move around by putting her knee in a chair and moving the chair in front of her to walk. With each step, she slowly gained strength, and her determination was a joy to see. My prayer was answered: her life was saved and her leg was restored!

One day, I looked out my window to see Cleautilde coming toward me, and she was wearing shoes! How I praised God for her health and for the obvious care she was now giving to her feet! When she reached me, she hugged me and cried, "You are my mama! You saved my life!" I talked with Cleautilde about the Lord again and reminded her of His mercy in the healing of her leg. She didn't accept Christ as her Savior while I was there, but I pray that she called on Him later in her life.

Near the end of our term in the Beni area, the idea of working in Peru had been on my mind. I mentioned it to George and we purposed to pray about it and wait to see how the Lord directed. Peru always entered our discussions as a consideration for our next work station, but no confirmation from the Lord was given to us.

After a few months of patiently praying, George came to me and said, "Ruthie, are you ready to tell me how you feel about the move to Peru?" He told me that if our answers were not the same, then Peru was not the place we should go. I was ready to give my answer and I said, "After much prayer, I believe Peru is the place for our next term." George responded that he felt the same. We experienced a great sense of peace about our decision. Now we would wait upon God's confirmation, knowing that wherever He led us, He would be there with us.

CHAPTER SIX

PERSEVERANCE

"Blessed is a man who perseveres under trial…"
James 1:12

When we arrived in the United States for furlough, George and I reported to our supporting churches and began the work of preparation for our new place of service. Since New Tribes Mission had no ministry in Peru, we resigned from that board and applied to serve under Maranatha Baptist Mission based in Natchez, Mississippi. The Lord was leading us to the village of Tushmo, Peru, a small village in the Amazon Basin. Here we would work with the Cocama people who had settled from upriver.

While in Natchez, we made plans for our children's schooling. We arranged for Rebecca and Bobby to attend a boarding school called the South American Mission School and for Louise to enroll in the Wycliffe Translator's School. These arrangements would allow them to be with us much more than when they were at Tambo. The Wycliffe base was close enough to allow Louise to live at home and walk back and forth to school. Rebecca and Bobby would live at the South American

Mission School during the week but would be close enough to come home every weekend.

The furlough passed quickly, and soon we were once again on our way to South America. Most of the available planes going to South American countries left late at night, allowing for little rest during the six-hour flight to Lima. Our very tired family collected our baggage and went through customs, then found a hotel room and got some much-needed rest. Later we headed to the government offices to get the necessary residential and identification papers we must have before moving on to Pucallpa. The village of Tushmo where we would be stationed was almost eleven miles east of Pucallpa. From there, we would be just a little over thirty miles away from the border of Brazil.

It was now time for Gilberto and Saul to report for military service in Bolivia. George would travel with them to Bolivia to assist them if necessary. Afterwards, he would take care of some other business matters and attempt to sell to other missionaries the items which we had stored before leaving for furlough. After completing these tasks, George would meet the rest of us in Pucallpa.

In the city, we would have electricity, running water, and other conveniences, but we had no contacts, no locations for possible assistance, and no one to aid us in finding a temporary residence here in Pucallpa until more permanent arrangements could be made in Tushmo. So where were we lost lambs supposed to start? As always, God supplied our need, this time in the form of the taxi driver who picked us up at the airport. When we explained our situation, the taxi driver immediately took us to a reliable hotel which was directly across the street from a clean restaurant. What a relief! Here in the hotel, the children could entertain themselves in safety while I searched for a suitable place to live. My only regret was that the kind, helpful Samaritan hurried off before we could properly thank him.

Gilberto's health issues had caused him to be rejected by the Bolivia military, so he and George met us in Pucallpa. George and I now searched for housing in Tushmo and at last found a place to rent. The agreement between George and the owner of the property was that our rent would be paid by the construction of a fence and the installation of a well. As soon as we moved, George and Gilberto erected a fence around the house, creating a safer place for us since stealing was such a common practice among the villagers.

We decided to hire two local men to dig the well. We watched as the men dug slowly due to the hard clay. Then began the stage of work where one man stood inside the hole, continuing to enlarge the well by shoveling dirt into a bucket which the second man pulled up to the surface to be emptied. This process was repeated until the digging reached softer soil. Eventually, the men began placing well tiles, about three feet wide by three feet in length, securing the sides of the well. As they dug around and under the edge of the tile, it kept sinking and they would add another tile, continuing this way until they reached sandy soil at about sixteen feet. Six tiles were sufficient with the top tile mostly above ground. The work of digging continued until the sand became wet and finally reached a water level of about two feet no matter how many buckets of water were removed from the well. Now we had a fence and a well, and our rent had been paid.

We all worked to adjust to the heat of the Amazon Basin and to the crowded conditions of our small rented home. The house had two petitions creating three rooms. One small portion was designated the girls' sleeping area. Bobby and Gilberto took another tiny section for their personal quarters, and George and I took the leftovers. With only three rooms in which to live and store everything, we experienced some moments of frustration and even desperation. The old galvanized roof was full of holes, so when it rained, everything had to be covered in plastic to prevent total drenching, but we enjoyed life in that tiny little space until we acquired a lot for building a bigger house about a year later. Our combined space had been about sixteen feet by sixteen feet, not leaving much space for sitting and visiting. A separate "building" with bamboo sides, a thatched roof, and a mud floor served as our kitchen. Here we placed our kitchen table which became our gathering place. For light at night, we used a gas lantern.

In the eyes of the Cocama people, our house was an exceptionally good house. Their homes typically had bamboo walls with a palm leaf roof and a floor made of palm tree trunks that had been split with a machete, while ours had thin rough unfinished wood walls. Their houses were raised off the ground on logs with notched logs providing steps to enter. They usually had only two rooms with mosquito nets providing the only privacy, while we had three rooms petitioned with unfinished wood. In most of their homes, a larger room was used as a living room, and the other room served as a bedroom for everyone in the family. Their kitchens were, like ours, small buildings out back of the main house. Sometimes there was a table to use for meals. If a family did not have a table, they sat anywhere they could find space to sit, talk and eat. Since there was no electricity, they made lamparinas to provide light at night. To make a lamparina, they took an empty condensed milk can with its hole in the top, added kerosene, and then inserted a makeshift wick down into it.

In Tushmo as in every other place we had lived, the Lord provided us with plenty of nutritious foods to eat. Vegetables did not grow well in the Amazon Basin, so a variety of vegetables and other supplies were shipped in by truck from Lima and other areas of higher altitude. A 500-mile road that ran from Lima over the mountains to Pucallpa enabled a large selection of food items, including powdered milk, to be purchased at the market. Fresh fruits from the surrounding area and those shipped from distant merchants provided a greater variety of fruits than could be found even in the United States. There was also plenty of fresh fish from the river and often fresh ronsoco (also known as capybara), a pig-like animal hunted in swampy areas at night, to add a tender treat to many of our meals.

By comparison, a typical Cocama family's diet consisted primarily of rice or yucca, fried bananas, and a fish if they lived near a river. If fish were not available for the meal, some animal from the jungle might be brought home following a hunting trip. A wild pig, tapir, ronsoco, wild turkey, jochi or maybe a monkey might grace the family table along with seasonal fresh fruit. It did not take long for us to discover that the villagers had great skill with seasonings for which we quickly developed a taste. A lighter meal was a green banana mashed up and seasoned, then boiled with plenty of liquid which thickened into a delicious dense soup.

We had been prepared to expect our work with the Cocama people to be difficult. Other missionaries who had worked with them had given up. No one had made any headway in their attempts to present the gospel. A Brethren missionary told us very bluntly that it was nearly impossible to reach the people with the good news of Jesus. He predicted, "You won't stay with the Cocamas long because they do not respond to the gospel." Upon hearing such discouraging news, our hearts were challenged, but we were also encouraged because we knew this would be the work of the Holy Spirit. We knew God had led us to Tushmo and we believed that He would complete what He had begun. We knew we were called to trust and to wait, and we cried out to God, asking for wisdom, help and guidance. We had been in the village for seven months with no response. This period in our lives was so difficult, but it drew us closer to God as we moved toward Him, seeking the comfort of His nearness.

During those seven months, God laid it on my heart to start sharing with the children of Tushmo. It was such a blessing to see how the children responded to the Bible stories told in my kitchen using flannel-graph figures. They loved them so much that they started bringing their mothers to the study. It was a small start, but it encouraged us, and we continued praying for wisdom.

We met many interesting people in the village, one of whom was Heraldo, a member of the communist party which was known in South America as "The Shining Light." I recalled a book written in Spanish entitled *The Mind of a Communist* and I offered it to him to read. As time passed, I noticed that he was changing his mind about some of his philosophies and ideas. I learned that he had begun to read the New Testament, and through the work of the Holy Spirit, Heraldo was saved. Praise the Lord! This man has been faithful ever since and is a person of great influence among the villagers.

Also very important to the life of the village was the mayor. George and I arranged to meet this important leader to open the channels of communication between us. During our meeting, George happened to ask the question, "What does the village produce?" Surprisingly, the mayor's response without a moment's thought was a resounding "Babies!" The truth of this statement was supported by my personal experience of delivering hundreds of babies during my years in Bolivia and Peru. George always said that I had delivered 2,200, but I think he exaggerated! However many it actually was, I have been told that it was considerably more than most obstetricians deliver during their practices. I have had the privilege of bringing babies into the Quechua, Tacana, Shipibo, Piro, and Cocama people groups, and I rejoice that at almost every birth, the good news of the gospel was shared with the families.

The village midwife attended many of the births and did a good job comforting and aiding the mother through the birthing process. She was by the mother's side throughout the birth, assisting her where there was usually no other medical assistance. She was proficient in many of the procedures of birthing, but she and I differed in some of our practices. She was accustomed to doing things her way, and she helped many mothers while they were giving birth. I preferred to give a little more attention to sanitation. No matter how careful we were in disinfecting, there could always be a chance of infection considering that the baby would be born on a dirty rough wood floor, on a dirty cement floor, or on a mud floor. In all the hundreds of births I attended, I remember only one with the mother in a bed. Most of our differences were preferences resulting from the differences in our training, and I appreciated her service.

Men often came to Tushmo to learn witchcraft where there were several practicing witches, each one eager to pass their skills on to younger men. One village witch named Raul lived only four houses down from us. Another witch doctor named Delphine lived in a house about a hundred feet from our home. We observed the many aspects of a pagan funeral when a relative of Delphine's died and the body was brought to his house for the wake. It was customary for the dead to be buried within twenty-four hours, during which time the family must buy wood, build a coffin, prepare the body, and console one another. People began to gather at Delphine's home. That night after dark, a cup of hot chocolate was served, and the visitors began making noises of all types. Drums could be heard as the people danced, screamed and yelled. Whatever they could think of to make noise became a part of the ritual, because they did not want the spirit which they believed caused the death to enter anyone else at the wake.

On another occasion, a young girl died. Her mother told the other villagers that the spirit of a boa constrictor had entered her child causing her death. We often saw customs that challenged us to pray fervently for the people's eyes to be opened to the need for abandoning their ancient customs. I recall seeing five ladies sitting around laughing and seemingly having a good time. They were sitting on the bare ground, chewing kernels of corn or peanuts. They would chew and chew and chew and then spit the contents of their mouths into a large clay container that had been placed in the center of their group. I realized that they were performing the "chew and spit method" for making their fermented drink to be used for the upcoming holiday celebration (*fiesta*). Water and sugar would be added to the mix and a cover placed over it to keep out insects and trash until the mixture was fermented and ready to drink- maybe not the best choice of drink considering how it was made!

The government provided a village school for the children up to sixth grade. If more education was desired after that, the people must travel to Pucallpa, although there were also some reading classes offered for adults in Tushmo. Most of the children could now read at least a little bit, and the adults were progressing slowly, but they clung tightly to their old customs.

In their homes, there was no running water and there were no inside toilets. After George and I built an outhouse, we noticed a few other villagers were building their own outhouses. The school also built outhouses for the children's use. The people made progress as they were able to afford it. Some of the women were able to purchase a sewing machine which enabled them to make some of their clothes. The women could attend classes to learn the skills of sewing. It then became important for a man to have a wristwatch which gave him an air of affluence. Then battery-powered radios started appearing in the homes.

The Cocama people loved to gather and visit with each other and this often led to trouble. At about five or six o'clock, the villagers often took walks together in the calm of the evening. The only problem was what developed during the walk. With quite a few people present, if there wasn't already a story about someone or another, there soon would be one, and the story would grow as the people walked. It seemed that telling the truth was more difficult than lying. George and I longed for the people to hear the Word of God and experience its power to change their lives.

There are two more interesting characters in the village I need to mention. The children loved pets and saved up their money to buy a little monkey. They certainly got their money's worth of fun from that little guy. It did not take long to discover that the monkey had a sweet tooth and a great love of oatmeal. Bobby started this love affair by giving him oatmeal with a little sugar on it. That little monkey would go absolutely crazy over it. As he dove hungrily into his treat, he performed a series of antics hoping to receive even more. The cup that was used as his feeding dish had only about an inch of oatmeal in it but when he finished, his face would be covered with cereal and sugar, causing us to wonder where it all came from! That mischievous little character kept things stirred up for he knew how to get into much more than cereal. Growing outside by the kitchen window was a bush loaded with small hot peppers, and he was drawn to the bright red color. One day his curiosity got the best of him, and before anyone knew it, he swiped one of those little red jewels. Before long, he was a very unhappy fellow with a very hot mouth. It must have been a learning experience for him, because he was not drawn to the bush anymore and he certainly did not eat any red peppers after that. Rebecca also added to the village population when she obtained a pet toucan. It was brightly colored and very pretty. The bird was very tame and allowed Rebecca to hold it and pet it. She really enjoyed her toucan and was sorry when it later died.

Living on the far side of the village were a couple of Piro families, a group of people not well-accepted by the Cocamas. One day a Piro woman came to me asking what could be done to help her child who was gravely ill. After the child received proper medical care, she recovered, and the mother began spreading the good news that the gringa (white foreigner) could help when a person became sick. This message became a door-opener as others began coming to ask for medical help. Along with the care they needed, they also received as much of the gospel message as we were able to share each time.

I was soon being summoned for as many as three births in a day. With good medical care, the mothers had fewer health issues during their pregnancies and the infant mortality rate dropped. As the villagers saw these results and grew to trust in my abilities, they began to view my time as their time. The Cocamas started their day early, usually at the crack of dawn, and they expected the same from George and me. Sometimes, they arrived before six o'clock in the morning! We found that when people have a need, especially an illness, they are more apt to listen to the story of Christ's love for them. In His time, God used the medical skills He had allowed me to learn while serving in Tambo to melt away the ice of indifference and unbelief.

Often there were challenges, but the Lord was faithful to give us wisdom. During births, I often had to turn the babies to head-first position. There were cross-section babies that if not turned could cause the death of the mother. There were often multiple births; I delivered twins and even triplets. One baby I recall very well weighed over ten pounds and the mother had been pregnant for ten months. This birth resulted in an episiotomy, but the baby was born healthy. As soon as he was delivered, his thumb flew into his mouth; he was hungry! Of all the births I attended, there were only two stillbirths and only two deaths. I am eternally grateful that God chose to allow me to serve in this capacity of helping mothers during birth and bringing joy to so many.

Not all cases called for medical knowledge; some called for a dose of common sense. Many moms often face what I call the bean-in-the-nose challenge. Such was the case one day when a mother came to me concerned about her three-year-old who had stuck a bean up his nose. It could not be retrieved by anyone in the family, so they brought him to me. Amidst wiggles, whines and grunts, I attempted to remove the bean. The child was obviously afraid, and when I moved toward him with my small forceps, a look of pure terror came over his face and an ear-splitting howl erupted. No one could calm him, and it was almost impossible for me to hold the child still to try to get the bean. As he cried and screamed, the bean scooted back and forth, ultimately moving farther up into the nose cavity. Finally, when everyone was exhausted and I was concerned that damage might be done to his nose, I gave the mother some advice to try at home. I told her to have him hold his breath and then to cover his mouth. She was to hold his mouth shut, forcing him to breathe out through his nose, hopefully dislodging the bean. I was glad to hear later that the child was beanless and had no sprouting fear of doctors!

Lacking training in everyday hygiene, the villagers could not understand that things that looked clean could make them sick. If a substance didn't look dirty, it was assumed to be safe to eat or touch. Germs were unknown to them, and this lack of understanding led to endless medical needs. Trench mouth was common in babies, and intestinal parasites and infections in adults and children were a daily part of my work. Good nutrition was not understood either. Even with good food available, mothers often gave their babies cornstarch and water in a bottle just to keep them quiet. I regularly treated babies that had developed pellagra, a disease caused by the lack of the vitamin niacin, due to malnutrition from a continuous diet of cornstarch and water.

Because of the growing need for medical help, I determined to go to the Ministry of Health in Lima to be registered as a health officer just as I had been in Bolivia. This would allow me to purchase medicines to be used in the village. With the authority to buy and disburse medications, the people of our area were able to be helped when they would not otherwise have been able to receive medical aid. Medications were purchased in bulk and kept on hand for the many medical needs. We never charged the villagers for my services, but they were expected to pay for the medications and medical supplies used during a procedure. The delivery of a baby usually cost ten cents or less. A shot of penicillin or streptomycin cost only ten cents.

I was kept busy attending medical needs and I enjoyed it. I spent a great deal of time studying the nursing books my friend had given me. When a case was extremely difficult, God gave me His wisdom and guidance, and throughout my medical practice, I learned my limitations while seeing the unlimited power of my God.

Some difficult cases stand out to me. A woman with very bad eyesight came to me asking for an operation to help her to see better. I had to explain to her that I was not a surgeon and could not help her. If she could find a way to go to see an eye specialist in the city, there might be help for her. I desired to help but was unable. Once, a man came with extreme hearing loss for which I could do nothing except check his ear and remove a buildup of wax. He left unable to hear. One man came with a twig in his eye. The twig was over 1/8 inch in diameter, and I had to refer him to a specialist in the city. I was just unable to help in such cases demanding special skills. Situations like these bothered me when I was unable to help, but I knew that God was still able to help them in spite of my limitations.

A lot and building had been secured for the church, and we could now put a door on a building where services could be held. There was great joy and excitement as the women of the church took on an important project: the building of benches. Men were not available for this task, because many of them were hunting in the jungle, and others were working at the Wycliffe translators' base. The few people who had accepted the Lord Jesus as Savior were baptized in a nearby lake. This was such a blessed time, the beginning of Iglesia Bautista de Tushmo (Maranatha Baptist Church of Tushmo). Praise the Lord! This had not happened overnight. God had heard our pleas and had accomplished this in His way and in His time.

Over time, George and I noticed that when villagers accepted the Lord as Savior and seemed to show potential for growth, distance would begin to develop between them and other believers. Most of the time we found that family or friends had begun to discourage and challenge their faith because they were no longer living in accord with their family's or friends' beliefs.

We had been in our little house for a little over a year, watching for a piece of land suitable for building a bigger house. We finally found a 50' x 100' lot which would allow space for a house with some left over for a yard. We continued our mission work as we began the preliminary work on our new home with priority placed on putting in a well for our own water supply. Next came putting up a fence for security. We decided to build an outhouse so that George would have a place to sleep on the property, something like a guard house, and the wood and supplies had been delivered for building the house. A temporary floor was put in the outhouse and seats would be added later.

Ordering the correct supplies was of great importance. George chose a hardwood called pumaquiro (tiger tooth) to prevent termites from destroying the house. (The workers were the first to experience the hardness of this wood. In order to drive a nail into it, they must first oil the point of the nail. If a nail bent, they learned to remove the nail and then use the same hole for the next nail.) After all the necessary supplies were ordered, we were ready to build a foundation on stilts so that torrential rains during the rainy season would not be a problem.

George, being from the heart of London, was not a handyman, but he had a willingness to help in any way possible. He often held the wood as someone else measured and cut it. Everything including drilling and sawing had to be done by hand, so George always found work to do. The studs went up, the foundation was laid, and the floor was built on hardwood posts slightly more than sixteen inches above ground level to keep termites out. We hired a local man from the village to put a galvanized roof on the house. Then we received the grand news that help was on its way. My home church where I had grown up in East Springfield, Pennsylvania, the Federated Church, was sending a group of people to help us build our home.

When these faithful workers arrived, we showed them around our village. They told us later that they were wondering where they would be able to stay. The best we could offer them was a few pieces of plywood for privacy as they slept on the floor that had already been completed. Everything was covered with plastic to prevent drenching from the tropical rains. Darkness arrived at about 6:30 p.m. all year, so kerosene lights, Coleman lanterns, and flashlights were used to continue working after dark. Sounds of their labor filled the air until our home reached its completion.

Ours was a very simple house. Sheets of plywood served as petitions and no ceilings were needed. We had doors on the bedrooms, but the closets had curtains instead of doors. Hardwood louver windows which were installed for security also kept rain out, and screens kept insects out as well. We had two bedrooms, a kitchen, a loft where the boys slept, and a living room. We now had plenty of room for the visitors who came daily for one reason or another, often with medical needs.

One funny episode occurred around our table when a young girl came to visit for a few days. She and I were sitting at the table enjoying a time of quiet fellowship when suddenly a small greenish-gray alligator dropped from the loft and landed right in front of my young guest. She screamed and waved her hands in an attempt to get the horrible thing away from her. From above came a roar of rambunctious laughter from two very mischievous boys. A bit of detective work revealed that the vicious intruder was made of rubber and was quite harmless. We all settled back down around our favorite gathering spot, the kitchen table, for a great deal of laughter.

Louise recalls how the children often flocked around her father, whom they called Grandfather. One favorite memory for Louise was watching the children race to get to their home and run in to play on the bright red carpet of the living room floor. Toys had been placed there for their enjoyment, and giggles and laughter filled the area of the bright red carpet, the area they considered their special playground with Grandfather.

A pitcher pump brought from Pennsylvania was mounted on a high landing off the stairway to the loft in the back room directly above the well. Having a fifty-five-gallon barrel to pump full each day gave us running water for the shower, a small washing area in back room, and the kitchen. We didn't need to heat the water for showers because the sun warmed the metal roof which kept the barrel warm all the time. Hot water was a treasure, not only in the showers but also in the kitchen. I had never asked the Lord for these conveniences, but when He gave them to me, my heart rejoiced.

Not long after we moved into our house, I heard a lady yell for me at the gate. I went out to see what she needed and found her in an agitated state, concern written all over her face. She told me to hurry to the house where Norma lived nearby. I dropped everything and ran there quickly, but Norma had already delivered her baby in the doorway of her home before I got there. She was just seven months pregnant, and her baby girl was premature and born on a mud floor without anyone in attendance. Since there was no incubator available, I explained the proper care for the little one. I stressed the importance of following the instructions for the sake of the baby's little lungs and nervous system. The directions were meticulously followed, and that baby is now the lovely wife of a pastor in the Andes Mountains.

Getting money exchanged was rather easy in Pucallpa. We could go to the bank with our statement from an American bank and receive Peruvian currency, but we sometimes chose to go through a commercial representative to receive a better exchange. On one occasion after getting the exchange, I went to the market to purchase a few items. When I started to pay, I realized that the whole month's support was missing from my purse. Someone had evidently waited outside the place of exchange, then followed me to the market. Even though I had kept my purse securely under my arm the entire time, the thief had managed to get its contents by slashing the back of it. That month we went without some things we normally would have had, but the Lord provided for us through the goodness of missionaries who heard what happened and felt led to help us.

George and I continued to pray for villagers to come to the Lord. The first young fellow who did was Alfredo. We met

Alfredo when he was about seventeen years old. We heard that he was sick because someone in the village had cursed him. The first time we visited him, all he would do was look away from us. We decided not to be discouraged but to continue visiting him. Eventually, he began to show interest in what we had to share. His health gradually improved, allowing him to attend our meetings. Before long, Alfredo heard the gospel and accepted the Lord. As George discipled him, he grew in his understanding of the Word and his daily walk with the Lord deepened.

Others who came to know the Lord faced persecution. Thomas was one whose wife constantly made things difficult for him as he attempted to grow in the Lord. Another man was a farmer who was married with six children when he came to the Lord. He grew in the Lord and was always in the church when he was in the village and not working in his fields. He eventually became a deacon in the church and was a dependable leader.

George often taught about how Jesus loves every one of us and died for us because we are sinners in need of God's forgiveness. One night, six boys about eleven and twelve years of age came to our house excitedly telling George about how they had been talking among themselves and now wanted to accept the Lord. What a blessing to have a part in leading all six of these boys to the Lord Jesus that night! Sadly, after a while, two of the boys lost interest and dropped out of the picture, but the other four were faithful to attend church services and to study the Bible.

For a time, one of the four boys, Moises Huaymacari, was not living like a Christian, but God was not through with him. Several years passed and the Lord began a work in his heart. As Moises got older, he matured in the Lord and eventually felt His call to become a pastor. His family was very poor, but the Lord provided the finances he needed to get his training and education. After seminary, he started a church in a small Quechua area up in the Andes Mountains, a remote area where he saw a great need for the gospel. Moises responded to God's call, taking no consideration for his own personal needs. He came from a hot, humid area to a very cold, frigid one. He had no blankets, no warm clothing, and the food was totally foreign to him. He obeyed the Lord and God blessed his efforts. The church he started now has more than one hundred regular attenders, and many have accepted Jesus as their Savior. We were blessed to see a glimpse of God's intricate workings in the lives of people, for Moises' faithful helpmate is Norma's premature baby whom I had been privileged to care for many years before.

Our second Christmas in Tushmo, George and I wanted to give Gilberto, Louise, Rebecca, and Bobby something special and had not yet thought of what that should be. It should be a gift to remember, something they would treasure. After much thought, the perfect gift idea came to me, if only it could be found. For weeks I looked and looked with no success. Just when I thought we would have to think of something else, I received a pleasant surprise. One day while in the city buying supplies, I saw the gift standing there in all its glory: a big bottle of ketchup. That's right, ketchup. All of our children loved ketchup. It was the perfect gift. I left the store with four bottles in hand and an extra bounce in my step. Who would have thought that a bottle of ketchup would please a child for Christmas? One was so glad to have it that the bottle was empty in no time. Another tried to make it last as long as it possibly could. All of them were thoroughly delighted! What fun we had watching their reactions to a simple bottle of ketchup!

Among our Cocama friends, some children received a Christmas present of some kind while others did not, depending on their family's financial situation. Gifts were usually a small doll for a little girl or a motorcar for a boy. The gifts were usually very cheap and did not last long. In school, older children found dried-up plants, cleaned off the dried leaves, and then decorated each little twig with tinfoil. The children were graded on the completed project. These simple activities made up all of the Christmas celebration the children experienced. And they were taught the real meaning of Christmas.

About two years after we arrived in the village, the village authorities had a meeting at which a vote was taken, the outcome of which approved me to start a medical post in Tushmo. After being presented with this offer, I accepted the responsibility on the condition that the village be responsible for constructing and furnishing the building. The leaders agreed and the villagers soon had a two-room facility built on a corner lot. One room was graced with a handcrafted desk and a rustic chair. Wycliffe Institute built a nice medicine and supply cabinet. The men of the village built a couple of benches where patients could wait comfortably until they were called for their examinations. The second room was the consultation and examination room. The medical post was to be opened three mornings each week. If there was an emergency, the people knew that they could come to our house where I would attend to their needs as well as I could.

Sometimes those who came for help were experiencing the results of their sinful life choices. Once some young men who were suffering from venereal disease came to us for advice, but they would not admit the wrong of their lifestyle which had led to the condition now destroying their lives. As we talked, I told them clearly that we will all reap the consequences of sin- spiritually, emotionally, and physically. I explained that the venereal disease was a direct result of their choice to be with a woman from the streets, and we cautioned them not to become sexually involved with another woman because of the risk of spreading the disease. This discussion provided a wonderful opportunity to talk about the gospel and to share the message of salvation. Our prayer for these men was that their eyes might be opened to see the truth, to turn from their wicked ways and accept Christ as their Savior.

Our children adapted well to life on the mission field and found many sources of entertainment. Soccer is very popular throughout South America, and every Sunday afternoon was soccer time for our boys. Gilberto wasn't a great athlete, but he loved to watch the games. Bobby had a natural ability for sports and was also extremely good at riding a bicycle. It came to our attention that Bobby had been entertaining the soccer game crowds at half-time by performing wheelies and various tricks. He also obtained a unicycle from a boy who had left to go back to the United States. Bobby spent hours practicing until he could jump, go backwards, and even go up and down stairs on the unicycle. All three of our children were excellent athletes and loved the outdoors. Louise often played soccer with friends, and she played a lot of volleyball. As a teenager, she played so well that she was asked to join a men's volleyball team with students from the Wycliffe Bible Translators Center. She enjoyed playing as a setter when they played in a men's league in Pucallpa once a week.

Not all of the children's experiences were light and happy. While Rebecca was in high school at the Wycliffe base nearby, she and a group of friends each paid their share of the fee to go to the boquieron, an area called Big Mouth, for a weekend. They found great places to swim surrounded by beautiful orchids that grew throughout the area. The young people were unaware that further up the river it had rained, creating a flash flood that was moving in their direction. Into their beautiful day rushed roaring, swirling waters which caught one of the girls and carried her away. The other boys and girls rushed to throw her a rope, but they were unable to reach her. Her body was recovered downriver a couple of days later, leaving a group of young people to contemplate the realities of life and death. Rebecca later told us that this tragedy gave her a great respect for water and caused her to swim with caution and awareness of her surroundings.

Bobby and Rebecca often went out in the canoe on Saturdays and spent the day fishing. They were both extremely good swimmers so George and I did not worry much. We knew they were relaxing and enjoying the lazy, laid-back fun of dropping a line in the water and waiting for a bite. During the rainy season and when the water was high, they could catch the small shrimp which were plentiful in our area. On one of these lazy Saturdays, Bobby and Rebecca had caught a good supply of shrimp when suddenly they found themselves stuck. Try as they might, they could not move that canoe. After some investigating, the two frustrated fishermen realized that the boat was stuck on a fence post, and in their struggle to free the canoe, all their hard-earned shrimp were lost. They were disappointed, but they came home bubbly about their day of mishap. On other more successful outings, the kids brought home fish which they roasted over an outdoor fire and shared with everyone in the family. We also had a gracious neighbor who fished and hunted for a living, so we almost always had fish in our kerosene refrigerator.

When I was invited by the authorities of the hospital in Pucallpa to join the efforts of the Yarina Cocha to inoculate children to prevent diseases such as whooping cough, measles, and mumps, I did not have to think about my decision. I immediately agreed to help. We made three trips about six weeks apart, and I enjoyed these visits to the villages and the opportunity to give inoculations to the children.

During the last round of vaccinations in Tushmo, I was called to deliver a baby at a house nearby. I was informed that the mother had been in labor for hours but was not able to deliver. Upon checking the position of the baby, I found that the baby was cross-section with its back to the birth canal. At this point, the other medical staff had finished the vaccinations and had now come to the house to observe my technique for the difficult birth. Immediately following the delivery, the leader of the group said to me, "Señora Rut, will you come and take charge of the maternity ward of the hospital?" Without hesitation I answered, "No, thank you, because I need to be here to help these people. If I go to the hospital, I will not be at hand to help them." I am sure the officials could tell that I meant what I said for they accepted my answer without protest.

Shortly after we finished the vaccine program, we heard that a woman in the village had been bitten by a rabid dog. Upon checking throughout the village, we found that other animals, including a pig and a cat, had also been bitten, and that meant the possibility of future victims. We knew that the villagers must be vaccinated against rabies. The doctor who brought the rabies vaccine to me instructed me in the procedure for administering it. I followed directions for each patient. I was surprised a few months later when an investigator came to our house to question me regarding the steps I had followed for the vaccinations. I related all that I could recall of the doctor's instructions. As a result of the investigation, the doctor was sent out of the area; he had given incorrect instructions regarding the dosage. Following his instructions, I had given only half of the dose that each one should have received. Several other people were bitten later, but, thankfully, not one person was diagnosed with rabies.

Rebecca had finished the eighth grade at the South American Mission School and had completed two years at the Wycliffe School. Louise was now in college in the United States. The Wycliffe School would be closing soon, so other plans must be made for Rebecca and Bobby's continued education. Two different families that we knew well from our years in Pennsylvania offered to have Bobby and Rebecca come to live with them while they attended high school. These were especially good arrangements because there was a son close to Bobby's age in the family that invited him and a daughter close to Rebecca's age in the other family. I went with the children to Pennsylvania and helped them get settled and then returned to Tushmo.

After Louise's sophomore year of college, she and a friend from school came to spend a couple of weeks with us. After the girls had settled in, we four made a trip to the Shipibo village. We felt sorry for Louise's guest because she was so fair that she sunburned easily. We enjoyed having them with us and Louise's friend got a good taste of missionary life.

Gilberto was such a blessing to us, always available to help with any task at hand. How we valued him and his faithfulness! After he completed his studies, his desire was to return to Bolivia and apply for a position teaching school. In order to do that, he must have his diploma certified. After seeking this documentation at the Ministry of Education in Lima, he was informed that his diploma would not be certified. After a period of discussion and then a lengthy wait, we were made aware that the staff wanted money before they would give Gilberto his certification. Of course, government officials are not supposed to be involved in bribery of any sort, but their actions-right or wrong- demanded a decision on our part. If Gilberto were to have his diploma certified, we would be forced to pay. Twenty dollars provided Gilberto with his official certified papers to present in Bolivia. He taught there many years and was a blessing to all who knew him. He was only forty-three when he had a heart attack and went to be with the Lord leaving a wife and three children. He had a servant's heart throughout the time he lived with us and indeed throughout his life.

During another furlough in 1977, George told me that he would like for me to stay in Pennsylvania with Bobby while he returned to the work in Peru. This would allow me to be with Bobby while he completed his senior year of high school and would also allow me to work on the reinstatement of my American citizenship. Before leaving Peru, I had spoken with the Consul General in the American Embassy in Lima, a person of great influence. She had attempted to find out how my citizenship had been lost, but after checking my records and other documents, she had been unable to discover when I could have lost my American citizenship. Now I determined with the Lord's help to do all that could be done to have it reinstated.

My friend Rebecca Williamson became the link to my rescuer, Senator John Stennis of Mississippi. Rebecca knew the Senator personally and she contacted him on my behalf. He was the head of Immigration and Naturalization Services at the time, and after hearing my story, he suggested that I write an affidavit, have it notarized, and mail it to his office. I did so and then received paperwork to be filled out and returned for processing. Then I waited. It seemed forever, but it had probably been only a month when I decided to contact the Senator's office to find out how things were progressing. I was horrified to be informed that my file was no longer being worked and had been moved to the "dead" files. When Senator Stennis learned of this error, he raised no small amount of ruckus and everyone in his office knew that my file best be found quickly! He later explained to my friend that a file placed in the dead files is usually there for good. My file, God be praised, was spared such a fate.

Though removed from the dead files, my file still bore the "Dead File" tag and soon found its way back waiting its burial. Once again, Senator Stennis, as soon as he was made aware of the mishap, came to the rescue and resurrected my file. Alas, I was still without my citizenship! I must wait on the Lord's timing.

At last, I received a notice to appear in Erie, Pennsylvania, with two witnesses on the following Monday morning at 9 o'clock. I received this notice on Saturday afternoon! I rounded up my birth certificate, driver's license, and everything else I could find that might help my case and hurried to arrange transportation.

I arrived in Erie on Sunday, and on Monday, I entered the courthouse with two friends who had agreed to be my witnesses. Shortly, I was called into chambers to be questioned. Then my witnesses were called to give testimony. Then we waited and prayed. After a short while, I was brought a paper to sign. The paper covered what I prayed was my certificate of citizenship which I believed I was being granted, but I wasn't sure. Then I returned home for more waiting.

Weeks passed before I finally received notification that I was to return to Erie where, with great emotion, I received the heartfelt honor of being sworn in as an American citizen on November 9, 1979. I was elated and overjoyed to be able to proudly proclaim, "I am an American citizen and I now have a certificate to prove it!" This was a definite answer to my prayers. Later, I discovered that I had been given incorrect information when I was told that I would not lose my American citizenship when I became a British citizen. I had never had dual citizenship at all. I didn't see anything wrong with being British, but it sure did feel great to be a proud American again!

Our children were all grown now, and my citizenship was restored, and it was time for me to be return to Peru with George where he was faithfully continuing to teach the Cocama people.

The Cocamas' idea of marriage was quite different from what George taught from the scripture. In their culture, the people had a big celebration of drinking and dancing, followed by everyone leaving the couple alone. The marriage would then be considered consummated and their life together would begin with no marriage ceremony. Seeing the need for the people to understand covenant marriage, George began teaching what God says about marriage. As a result, couples began to be married legally in the town office and then returning to church for another service before God. George could see that the people were learning they should conform to the laws of the land as well as to the law of God. Once when George performed the wedding ceremony for a young couple, an older couple who attended decided that they, too, should be married. This encouraged their daughter and her "husband" to marry, and their granddaughter and her "husband" also chose to follow their example. What a blessing it was to have a triple wedding for this family!

George and I had been looking forward to our wedding anniversary and we wanted to do something really special. We decided to go to Pucallpa and have a nice dinner in a restaurant, something we did not often do. We got all dressed up for our night on the town and happily climbed onto our only means of transportation at that time, our motorcycle. We headed toward Pucallpa looking forward to a special time together. Arriving in the next village, Yarina Cocha, we found that the villagers had been working on the road and there was now a deep ditch that extended across the whole width of the road. How could this be happening? Would we have to cancel our dinner? With some effort, George and I found a way around the ditch and continued into town. Having a nice meal together with time to talk quietly for a while was such a rarity, and we greatly enjoyed ourselves. Too soon, it was time to head home.

Back on the motor, we travelled quickly in the dark on that strange road. Here in Peru, there were no markers, no flares, and no signs anywhere along the crude road. There was absolutely nothing to warn of danger. Suddenly, I remembered the ditch! I stopped abruptly and swung the bike, and as we looked around us, we discovered that our bike had stopped on the very edge of that huge ditch. Peering over the edge, our hearts sang praise to God for His merciful hand of protection.

The next morning, I headed for town to do some grocery shopping, again on the motorcycle. As I approached the village of Yarina Cocha getting near where the ditch was located, I saw that I would need to go up a small hill. I climbed that hill and was making a right turn when my motorcycle frame broke, leaving the bike in two pieces. There I sat with only the chain holding those two disconnected pieces together. I must have made quite a sight as I sat on the back part of the bike, stretching my whole body forward, desperately holding on to the handle bars. I was embarrassed because startled people were all around me, attempting to solve the mystery of what had just happened. I realized that the frame had cracked from the strain of the abrupt stop as we swung around to avoid landing in the ditch the evening before. Soon, a truck came by, going in the right direction, and I stopped it and asked the driver for help. He agreed to take me and my motorcycle into town where I could arrange to have the bike welded. The repairman was able to work on the bike right away and was able to repair it by putting a metal bar in the frame so that it was now stronger than it was before the incident.

I was asked to go see a young fellow named Miguel Gonzales when he was nearly at the point of death. He was very weak and pale, suffering from a great number of intestinal parasites. I gave him an effective medication which led to his ultimate recovery. After hearing the gospel, Miguel showed a sincere interest, and George had the privilege of leading him to the Lord. Miguel started reading the Bible, and when he went into the army, he took his Bible with him. While in the military, he held Bible studies with other soldiers and earned the respect of the officers. After his release, he came to us, saying that he had set a goal of visiting every household in his village of San Lorenzo. By this time, he had a good knowledge of the Bible and was faithful to come to George for advice. He started having Bible studies in his village which was just a little less than a mile from ours. Our church in Tushmo desired to encourage Miguel's folks by giving them some benches if they could find a building in which to meet and they started having Sunday morning services. On a few occasions, our church went to theirs and shared services. Miguel was faithful to God and his congregation. A young pastor who was looking for a church came to San Lorezno, giving Miguel the opportunity to go to seminary. He became a very good preacher and the Lord used him greatly in other areas of the country in evangelistic meetings where many people accepted the Lord as their Savior. To this day, he is faithfully preaching the Word of God. He is not afraid to preach about hell and how to escape going there when you die, and he faithfully presents the plan of salvation and Jesus' sacrifice on the cross which makes it possible for those who accept Him as Savior to be with Him in heaven.

Our hearts were broken any time we saw a downward spiral in the life of one of our church members but especially when the individual was called to be a pastor. When our first term in Peru was completed and it was time for our furlough, George and I had prayed for guidance to select a man of God to leave in charge of overseeing the church in our absence. The man we felt God led us to give this responsibility was a man who had earned our trust, confidence and respect as a fellow Christian. George and I left at peace that the fellowship was in good hands and would receive good care from this pastor. At first, we received word that he was taking good care of the church, but later, George learned that he had begun to fail to prepare for church services.

Finally, he stopped holding services at all until he heard that George and I would soon be back. Then, he resumed services to give an appearance that he had been faithful. His attempt to deceive was apparent. Soon, he stopped attending church altogether. His testimony continued to weaken due to his increasingly worldly lifestyle. He eventually moved away from Tushmo, and we heard later that his home had been burned. The church members were discouraged and disappointed and needed a great deal of encouragement, but many of those who had drifted from the church returned. George faithfully encouraged the believers and gradually renewed their trust.

After we had been in Tushmo four or five months, a pickup truck that we had purchased before leaving for Peru arrived. That vehicle made travel so much easier for us, making it possible to reach more villages. Our hearts sang with excitement and anticipation as we loaded the truck with a projector, a generator, an extension cord, a couple of light bulbs and a bedsheet for a screen. Now with the film, *The Burning Hell*, which we had previously purchased, we had all that we needed for our presentation. Prayer, the greatest necessity of all, was issued up to the Giver of all blessings, and soon we found ourselves on a long dirt road on our way to show the film in many villages. We traveled off the main highway, into the villages away from the cities.

We had prepared a tentative schedule for the presentation of the film. As we entered each village, we looked for the school and then obtained permission to show the film before setting up for the presentation. In every village, as we began nailing up the sheet for the screen, this simple task drew the children and they had many questions. We liked this because they became our public relations crew, going forth, telling everyone- fathers, mothers, grandparents, aunts and uncles- that there was going to be a film that night when it got dark. Another asset for the promotion of the film was the electrical cord and bulbs, for we found out that lights helped to draw a crowd. Finally, out came our megaphone which we used to announce the time and the presentation.

After the presentation of *The Burning Hell*, an opportunity to receive Christ as Savior was given. Encouragement was always given to those who were saved to help them mature and grow in their knowledge of the Word of God. New converts were encouraged to attend an evangelical church as soon as possible if they could find one. Finally, each convert was given a Bible so that they could learn more about their God and be able to grow in their walk with Him. Sometimes villagers told us that the film had made them think but they were reluctant to accept the Lord as Savior. We were always kept busy answering questions after the showing of the film.

When the film was shown among the Shipibo people, there was a very good response. These people are a matriarchal group and the women responded first when the invitation was given, leading the way for the men. Sixteen men and women accepted Christ as their Savior one night. On another night in a different village, nine were saved. Sometimes fewer responded, but the Lord always worked through this film to change lives.

Traveling into higher altitudes to reach some of the mountain villages meant that the timing on the vehicle had to be set higher to give it more power for going up the steep roads. We were traveling up the road that leads to Huancayo, stopping in every little village to show the film. In England, George had ridden a bicycle everywhere and so had never learned to drive. I enjoyed driving usually, but I found steep and very narrow roads to be a challenge. Now as we moved further up into the hills, the road became increasingly steep, and I realized that something was wrong with our truck; we must stop. We were in a very dangerous place. We had been previously warned that others traveling this road had been robbed or killed in this very area. Near the road where we stopped was a company of men working. We had sat there only a few minutes when one of the men approached us, inquiring about our trouble. He began to check around the truck, and we were uneasy, not knowing his intentions. Finally, he told us that the coil was burned out. He left, and George and I then stood together while George prayed that God in His mercy would send someone to tow us into a village where there was a vehicle repair shop.

I started looking along the side of the road for something that would serve for towing the truck. We wanted to be ready when God answered our prayers. I soon found a long piece of cable and had just gotten back to George and the truck when two American men pulled up to ask how they could help us. Praise be to our God Who is our help in the midst of trouble! "God is our refuge and strength, a very present help in trouble" Psalm 46:1. Our help had come without delay and we were out of danger in a very short time. The men soon had the truck ready for towing and we were once more on the move. After leaving us at a garage where the truck could be fixed and after receiving our heartfelt gratitude, our rescuers were once again on their way to Lima.

Now that we had a working vehicle again, we were on our way to the next village where there continued to be a good response to the Word. In many areas when people were saved, we were begged to stay and teach them about the Lord. This is evidence that "the harvest is plentiful, but the laborers are few" Luke 10:2. Our hearts went out to them, lifting up prayers on their behalf.

We ended our journey in the city of Huancayo since we knew a pastor there. Again, there was a very good response to the message of the film and many individuals were saved. Visiting with the pastor was a true blessing for George and me.

He had gone to seminary to become a priest, but after finishing his training, he was saved and became a great caring pastor. His church was growing, and souls were being saved. After a wonderful time of fellowship with him, George and I headed back to Tushmo. Going down the road, we sang praises to our Almighty God for this wonderful trip that had added over sixty souls to the Shepherd's fold.

Now again on the road back to Tushmo for a couple of hours, I decided I wanted to stop and buy some of the delicious cheese the people made up in the mountains. It was not unusual for a young boy or girl to stand by the road calling out, "Queso, queso," (cheese, cheese) while holding high a pan filled with the cheese I so desired. It just so happened that this portion of the road was rather level for about 300 feet. We bought some cheese and were returning to the truck when we happened to look down and see a long streak of oil in the road, and it led from our vehicle. George determined that it was brake fluid and that the screw that held the fluid in the line had worked loose. I was thankful that I had thought to put brake fluid in the truck before we left Tushmo, but with the screw missing, how were we going to keep from losing fluid? Maybe we could follow the trail of oil to find the screw. Sure enough, we were able to follow the trail to the screw and were able to put it back in place.

Farther ahead, the road looked bad. It had rained and the road had been washed away. To go any farther meant that we would have to go over that area where the asphalt was still present but there was nothing under it to provide support. The road was on the cliff side so there was no way to go around the damage. We would have to go over the damaged section of the road. Hugging the mountainside, I gunned the engine so we could cross the weakened area quickly. We felt the need to lift our backsides up off the seat so there wouldn't be as much weight pushing down as we passed over the washed-out place.

After crossing that spot safely, we began to relax and to thank the Lord that the asphalt held us. We also had a very good laugh at ourselves for thinking it would help make it lighter to hold our backsides off the seat!

We were now in our second term in Peru. Louise, Rebecca and Bobby had all finished school and were working, Louise and Rebecca in Birmingham, Alabama, and Bobby in Jackson, Mississippi. A few weeks after our trip presenting the film, we received a message that Bobby had been in a serious car accident and was in intensive care in Jackson. Our immediate reaction was to place him in God's hands and then move quickly to make travel arrangements for me to go to him. During my preparation to leave, a constant prayer was going forth on behalf of our son. Not knowing how badly he was hurt or even if he would survive his injuries, we were praying every moment, and God's peace sustained us during this terrible time of not knowing.

When I arrived in Jackson, I was met by a kind lady who took me straight to the hospital and made it clear that she was there to assist me and expected no compensation for her service. Bobby responded well to his excellent medical care and was soon released from the hospital, and I then returned to Peru. We thank God for this time in our lives, for it reminded us that "…God causes all things to work together for good to those who love God, to those who are called according to His purpose" (Romans 8:28).

While I was away, the villagers had noticed that George took great care to avoid any appearance of wrong behavior. In that culture, the women expected that their husbands would find someone else for intimacy if they must be away from home for any length of time. The people had noticed that George had been very careful not to have any woman inside the house. If a woman came to the door, he talked with her on the porch. He never allowed himself to be alone with a woman under any circumstances, therefore allowing no room for harmful rumors to begin. The women came to tell me that my husband was a real gentleman and that he never had a woman in the house when I was not there. I had never given a thought to any such improper behavior, because I knew George was a man of integrity. I knew that he was like the overseer described in Titus 1:7-9: "above reproach as God's steward, not self-willed, not quick-tempered, not addicted to wine, not pugnacious, not fond of sordid gain, but hospitable, loving what is good, sensible, just, devout, self-controlled, holding fast the faithful word…"

While working in the medical post, I began to talk with the people about the need for a better building in which to meet the medical needs of the village. The first building had been rather crude with its thatched roof and its bamboo sides. The village needed a more stable building, one that could not be broken into easily. The years had passed and finally the village leaders were beginning to see the importance of building a new secure medical facility. Plans were now in the making and I was rejoicing.

It seemed with each step of progress came a greater demand for more. Then finally came a push to get electricity in the village. To receive electricity, each house had to have its own pole. When the wiring was up, each house was charged according to how many bulbs the house had, usually one to three. With the coming of electricity came modern conveniences. The women now had electric irons and maybe a refrigerator. Finally, the television made its appearance. Can you believe it? Television sets in the middle of the Amazon Basin! Once while I was out on the lake going to a Shipibo village, I looked up and could not believe what I was seeing. There was a television antenna sticking out of the top of a tree!

George was now teaching the scriptural principle regarding the church's responsibility to financially support a pastor. In most cases, the pastors of small churches had to find other work to meet their financial needs. George had often said that he wished to stay on the field as long as he could, but he was now seventy-five years old, and he no longer had the strength of his youth. He felt that it was time for us to return to the United States. We had peace about doing this, because we had served with these people for years and believed that they now needed to take more responsibility. George felt comfortable about leaving the ministry of the church in the care of a pastor, one who had accepted the responsibility of taking over the teaching and training of God's people. The Lord sent a man who had seminary training and had had a pastorate.

We began to prepare for the move by selling the film and the equipment used for showing it. So much had been accumulated through our years of service, but it was a rather easy task to dispose of it all. It was difficult to leave, realizing that we would no longer be stationed there and the people had become part of our lives, but we realized that the Lord understood the whole situation and we must leave every detail in His hands. George and I said our goodbyes and began our journey to the mission headquarters in Natchez, Mississippi, where we were welcomed to a new phase in our walk with God.

CHAPTER SEVEN

ENDURED

"...we count those blessed who endured..."
James 5:11

After spending thirty years on the mission field, it was difficult to hear George say, "Ruthie, I think we had better think of going back to the States and let a younger missionary do the work because I just cannot keep up with things anymore." I accepted the wisdom of this decision, partly because I knew of his health issues, but mostly because I knew that he had not made this decision without much prayer. It was also easier to accept, knowing that we would continue to serve wherever God allowed us to be.

It was 1986 and we were being welcomed by the staff of The Maranatha Baptist Mission Headquarters in Natchez, Mississippi. As we entered the facility, big, colorful posters and personal greetings assured us that we were at home. We now were resting in God's assurance that the work in Peru would continue in the hands of younger and stronger men and women and that He still had work for us to do. I was to work in the office as a receptionist while George served in various ways that allowed him to work at his own pace. About a year later, a need arose in the printshop, and I requested a transfer. I never thought I would be a printer, but I was printing for the Lord's work.

While in Peru, I had delivered a baby named Timmy whose right leg and hip were severely deformed. He was now four years old and had been unable to receive help for his condition. We began to seek help here in the USA. After we were referred to the Shriner's Hospital, we called and explained Timmy's situation. The Shriners then contacted a gentleman who agreed to be his sponsor. All that remained now was to get Timmy to Mississippi from Peru- no small task. Peru did not permit children to travel without a parent. Since both of Timmy's parents wanted to travel with him, this would require three plane tickets, an expense that we could not afford. We turned to Samaritan's Purse for help, and arrangements were finally made to bring Timmy and his parents to the United States.

When they arrived, we found that there would be a two-week wait to see the doctor before Timmy could begin his care at the Shriners' Hospital. It was the third week of October, the peak time of the fall season and the perfect time to take our Peruvian visitors on a northern sightseeing trip. As we drove northward, the whole countryside seemed to erupt with color. In every direction, we witnessed a beautiful splash of bright fall color. It was as if God had painted a picture of beauty just for this small boy and his parents who had never dreamed of such loveliness. In open-mouthed amazement, the father suddenly exclaimed, "Flowers, flowers, flowers! Flowers are everywhere!" Never having seen such brilliantly colored fauna, he had assumed the leaves to be flowers! As our guests were awed by the brightly colored leaves, George and I considered how often we had taken these blessings for granted. We continued to my sister's home in Pennsylvania where we spent a few days before traveling back south to the mission. We then returned home to wait for Timmy's appointment.

The day came for Timmy to be evaluated, and after many X-rays and thorough examinations, the doctors concluded that his foot would need to be amputated. The upper leg bone would then be fused to the lower bone, making his left leg to the knee the same length as that portion of his right leg. He could then be fitted with a prosthesis which would allow him to walk normally. It was difficult for his parents to agree to an amputation, but after consideration and with our encouragement, they gave their consent for the surgery.

The surgery was done, and Timmy was now recuperating in the hospital. He passed the time by looking out his window, watching birds or whatever passed by. One day, he thought he saw something fall. Looking again, he was surprised by something he had never seen before. "Mother," he said, "look outside. Feathers are falling. Feathers, lots and lots of feathers!" Putting aside her embroidery work, Timmy's mother stood and took in the scene for a moment. Taking a deep breath and then releasing it, she exclaimed, "This must be that snow they talked about!" The two watched in quiet amazement as the flakes became heavier and bigger. The next day, someone found a warm jacket for Timmy, and nurses wrapped his lower body in a blanket and placed him in a wheelchair. Off they zoomed down one corridor and then another until out the door they went into a winter wonderland. Snow covered everything and Timmy experienced another wonder of God's creation. The other children and nurses, laughing as they came, put snow in his hands and showed him how to make a snowball, and, yes, he soon found out how to use a snowball.

After several weeks, Timmy was released from the hospital to our home where he would wait for his prosthetic leg. During his time with us, he learned that a train came by the back of the house every day and he listened eagerly for it to come. Each day, one of us took him out to wave to the engineer as the train passed. After a while, the engineer took an interest in Timmy and came to our house one day to see him. Timmy was so pleased to have this honor! The engineer had come just to see him! Another pleasure for Timmy was seeing Santa at Christmas. As Santa came through our neighborhood on a pickup truck, he threw a delighted Timmy a fistful of candy. Timmy understood the real meaning of Christmas and the story of Jesus' birth, but he still enjoyed the attention from Santa.

During this period of waiting, there was plenty of time for conversation in our home, and we talked often about the Lord. The highlight of Timmy's visit was his acceptance of the Lord Jesus as his Savior one evening as George and I shared with him.

At last, the call came that the prosthesis was ready and we drove to the hospital for the fitting. Timmy had to learn which leg to use first to go upstairs and to remember to use the other leg to go downstairs. We rejoiced that when the time came for him to return to Peru, he would be able to stand and walk as easily as other children.

It was now August 30, 1989, and we had been home for more than two years. George had finished work at the mission for the day and had decided to walk home. It was a very hot day but George loved the outdoors and enjoyed walking, so he left early and started toward home about two miles away. Our mission founder's wife happened to be going somewhere along George's route and stopped and offered to take him home. When he got into her car and she could see him better, she became concerned. He was unusually red-faced from heat and was feeling terribly tired. When I arrived home, he was still extremely red and was resting, something out of the ordinary for him. I watched closely but could not determine what the trouble was. After the evening meal, I asked him how he was feeling. He answered, "Okay,

I'm just tired." When he went to bed much earlier than usual, I began to be very concerned. Something was definitely wrong, but I did not know what.

Just before dawn, George woke me and asked me to take him to the hospital. Entering the building, George told the first person in hospital attire that he thought he had just had a heart attack. The doctor's exam confirmed this, and X-rays revealed that the back side of his heart had been damaged. He would need open heart surgery right away. During his stay in the hospital, he comforted me and everyone around him by singing hymns of praise.

Even in his suffering, George was thinking of others, specifically of Timmy. He knew that the boy would still need special care and exercise for his leg when he returned home. He told me to make sure Timmy would have a bicycle to take back to Peru. I did not hesitate to find that bike, a pretty blue one. When I told George about Timmy's joy over his new bike, he was so pleased and a big smile of contentment spread across his tired face. I did not know then that this was our last moment together.

The following Saturday, September 2, 1989, Timmy's family and I went out early to search garage sales for items they could take back to Peru. As we returned home, the phone was ringing. When I answered it, a voice informed me that George, my dear partner in life, was now with the Lord. I immediately rushed to the hospital. His nurse told me his passing had been fast. She had just left him and as she passed the monitor, she could see that something was wrong. Rushing back to him, she found he had already gone. I was now without my husband of 34 years. Even in my grief, I was thankful that he had not suffered long.

Years ago, my father had purchased cemetery lots for the family, and, at my request, George would be buried there awaiting my future burial beside him. I would travel to East

Springfield, Pennsylvania, for his burial, leaving Timmy and his family with Spanish-speaking friends of ours in Natchez.

Louise, Rebecca and Bobby came to East Springfield from Mississippi and Alabama, and George's sister Violet and her husband flew from Canada. Many precious friends and a few missionaries came to offer their love and comfort. All had come to offer their respect to this godly man who had given his life in service to his Lord Jesus Christ. The service took on an air of special sweetness as George's voice began to fill the room of the funeral home. He had often sung in church and occasionally his solos were recorded. In planning the service, I decided to use these recordings during the memorial. George would sing at his own funeral! It was strange to hear his strong voice at this time, but the children told me later how much more personal and comforting the service became as they heard their father's voice once again praising the Lord.

I returned to Natchez very soon after and just a few weeks later, it was time for Timmy and his parents to return to Tushmo. Suitcases were packed, the bicycle was crated, and everything was loaded into the car for a drive to the airport where I saw them off to Peru. I stayed in touch with the family and heard that the bicycle provided good physical therapy for Timmy, just as George had foreseen. Timmy and I still correspond occasionally. He teaches religion in public schools in Peru and often presents the news on a radio station in Lima. He is also a part of a musical group which sings and plays gospel music in churches and other venues. George would be so pleased to know that his young friend has grown to be a godly servant of the Lord.

After Timmy's family left, the house felt empty. My work at the printshop kept me busy, but I worked alone and then went home alone. I had decided not to make any big decisions for a year, but as time passed, I recognized that being alone so much was not good for me. I needed to be with people and I knew that

I had to do something about it. Not wanting to make a quick decision, I put into practice a lesson George and I had learned on the mission field: I prayed and I waited.

I was sure that I would continue in God's call for me as a missionary, and in time, He guided me to Source of Light Mission International (SOL) in Madison, Georgia. This mission printed Bible studies beginning with salvation and going through growth as a Christian. Here I would work with other missionaries most of the time and would even live close to others on mission property. After being accepted, I moved from Natchez to Madison where I was assigned to the printshop. When I had been there a short time, the director of the Spanish department was asked to go to Chile to find someone to serve as the Field Director for that country, and I was asked to take her position. The Madison Correspondence School was comprised of the French, English and Spanish departments, as well as another department for prisoners, serving the many in prison who were studying our Bible courses.

This work was right up my alley and I thoroughly enjoyed it. I was blessed by fellowship with missionary friends with whom I worked daily and with the people who came as volunteers to help with the work. SOL printed Bible lessons in many languages to be sent throughout the world. Sometimes volunteers came as a group, but often a couple or a single person came to help. We were always blessed by our volunteers.

I had been at SOL almost five years when a retired gentleman who had lost his wife to cancer came to volunteer. Bob had been widowed for a short time, and he was having trouble with loneliness. He started coming every month to volunteer for a week, and we got acquainted during that time. He enjoyed the work at the mission, and I took note of his kindness and his love for people, especially children. I saw that he had a soft side. He had a tender heart and was very generous not only with money but also with his time whenever there was a need. His love of missions especially drew my attention. He enjoyed sharing the Word so much that he became a member of Gideons International, the organization which had given me a New Testament when I was a young girl. After spending time together during his visits to volunteer at the mission, Bob proposed.

Wedding bells rang on November 25, 1995, when I became the bride of Mr. Robert "Bob" Cornwell. For a while, we lived in a house trailer in the mission housing area. Bob now worked full-time at the mission, no longer needing to make a monthly 408-mile trip. He enjoyed working in the shipping department packing the Bible lessons and tracts to be sent all over the world. I had just started a SOL associate school in Spanish called Living Waters.

Bob didn't like living in the housing area, so we soon moved to a farmhouse that had previously been a cotton plantation home. We enjoyed that home, especially having people stay with us when they came to the mission. One of the memorable times was when the mission had an International Conference with missionaries coming from all over the world. We hosted a couple from Chile and had so much fun with them! That week gave us the opportunity to meet people from many other countries, including the King and Queen of Nigeria who were Christians and were attending the conference.

We were so encouraged with the progress of Living Waters that we felt free to take a short mission trip in the summer of 2000. Bob and I had the privilege of going to Tushmo, Peru, where George and I had worked. This trip allowed Bob to see firsthand what the Lord had done among the people that George and I had been told were impossible to reach with the gospel. It was such a blessing for me to see everybody again! Together we saw how the church was progressing and we encouraged them to be faithful to their Lord. The church building in the village had suffered damage from the termites and powder beetles that had made their home in the aged wood. The villagers hoped one day to have a building that could not be damaged by bugs. Our hearts told us that our next mission trip would be to return with a group and work together with the people to build a brick building for the church.

At home, I continued with Living Waters, sending, receiving and correcting lessons in Spanish. I stayed busy answering questions and counseling since the students sometimes wrote to me about their problems. The greatest blessing came when students wrote back to me telling me that they had accepted the Lord Jesus while taking the Bible courses. Praise the Lord for many souls that were saved through those Bible lessons!

In 2002, we returned to Tushmo with Fred Jordan from Augusta, Georgia. We dug and poured a foundation and were ready for the team of workers who joined us a week later. A group of seventeen, most from the Federated Church of East Springfield, Pennsylvania, arrived to help in the construction of a new brick church building that would not be susceptible to termites and beetles. Pastor Butch Lee of Sandy Creek Baptist Church of Madison headed up the construction and a great deal of work was accomplished under his supervision.

Before we left the United States for Tushmo, we had collected about 600 pairs of used eyeglasses and Bob's eye specialist had shown him how to check a person's eyes for a fitting. Word spread quickly in Tushmo that we had eyeglasses for those in need of them. At four o'clock in the morning, people began arriving from four different villages to stand in line to have their eyes checked. While the men worked on the construction, the ladies helped with the eyeglass project.

Later, the girls went out into the village to give out gospel tracts and to invite people to church. They also held meetings for the small children where they shared about the life of Christ. We all enjoyed a special treat from a young national lady who felt led to encourage us. Every day, she brought her delicious sweet rolls for all the workers. Another blessing to our group was a man known as Mr. Agua. He was very popular with the ever-thirsty work crew because he took on the job of supplying water for them. My sister Martha went with us on this trip and was stirred to say, "Now I see why you were anxious to get back on the field."

In 2004, we were able to return with a team of workers, mostly from Sandy Creek, and my sister Martha also went with us again. Our previous trips had been very difficult for Bob who suffered from altitude sickness. This time, he decided to stay home but was very supportive of me and the others who were able to go. The building for the Maranatha Baptist Church at Tushmo was completed. It was designed to seat one hundred and eighty people, and when it was completed, at least four hundred people came to dedicate it.

While in Tushmo on this trip, we saw another need in the village of San Lorenzo about three-fourths of a mile away. There the villagers had a small church building that had been damaged by termites and then had been destroyed by a strong wind. The remaining pieces had been put back up with extra supports added. It was a very simple structure with three sides closed in and a thatched roof to cover it. We knew we would come back to help meet their need of a sturdier building.

In 2006, we returned with a few workers from the US and several men from Tushmo to join the men of San Lorenzo to build a new place for them to meet. Before the work was complete, heavy rains caused a delay in the construction. The boys quickly changed into shorts so they could have a good shower under the eaves of the house where they were staying. Eventually, the rain stopped and the work was continued but was not completed until two years later when we returned to help finish the building. Glass was never used in windows in this hot climate, so rebar was used for security. The rebar was heated and twisted into an attractive design and it gave a finished appearance to the church building. A beautiful dedication service was held the night before we returned home. This service was led by our friend Miguel Gonzales whom George had led to the Lord long ago in Tushmo. Our hearts rejoiced as we crowded inside for the service of praise. At least a hundred people celebrated outside as they gathered around the windows.

On another occasion, Bob and I and two couples from the Sandy Creek Church went to Chile to help in a work program in prisons. A Chilean missionary with SOL had been working as Field Director for the country of Chile and also had an Associate School. Some of his students were prisoners. This led to prison officials and city officials being invited to a special event of awarding diplomas for finished Bible courses followed by a baptismal service.

Our group went to another prison for women where I had the privilege of giving the message. I spoke on forgiveness and six women raised their hands during the invitation. The women were very emotional and filled with remorse over their sin. One of them confessed that she had killed her husband and her children. Her repentance was very evident, and we rejoiced as she prayed to receive God's forgiveness. What a blessing!

The prison allowed children to stay with their mothers if relatives were unable to care for them. Each morning the children left the prison to attend public school. The prison also offered a very good rehabilitation program, providing training in skills they could use when released from prison. Some of the women made pretty jewelry boxes. Others sewed curtains and sheets which were sold in local stores. In addition to visiting the prisons, we visited schools where we presented the message of salvation.

We also had the privilege of visiting the Payunge Church, a church that we now call "the miracle church." We spent an afternoon out playing in the snow on a mountain and learned that the mountain erupted the very next day! On the night before we left, Chilean field directors Guillermo and Vicky Salazar invited our group to a special folk dance presentation by the couple who had won first place in the National Dance Competition. Dressed in colorful attire, they spun and twirled to the rhythm of the music, and it was easy to see why they were the winners of the competition. It was a perfect ending to our trip.

Later we learned that the Payunge Church faced a dilemma. Their land had been given to them by a farmer who had not handled the paperwork correctly. When he later sold his property, they were told that they would have to remove their building. God solved this problem in a very interesting way. Because of the rains during the rainy season, there was a great landslide which covered with mud the nearby road that led up into the mountains. Guillermo Salazar owned a vacant lot near the ocean, and he offered it to them. They were able to move the dirt from the road to his lot to build it up. Then they lifted the building onto logs and pulled it with oxen to move the "miracle church" to its new location. This was God's work! He moves at the right time to provide for our needs. He made the landslide, and He put the dirt on the lot, preparing it for the church building to be placed there.

Now we were back at home in Georgia where Bob had the task of maintaining our property, including the mowing of our very large yard. He had a hard time with allergies and a harder time keeping up with the yardwork. We had been in the farmhouse about two years when he came in one day, saying,

"Ruthie, I think it's time we lived near one of the kids. You know, we are getting older and these allergies are really bothering me." We began our search for a new place to live and did not have to search long before we found a house in the Birmingham, Alabama, area near my oldest daughter, Louise.

In Alabama, I continued my work with the Associate School, but I began to have some troublesome symptoms. My hands shook for no apparent reason, my balance was bad, and I often dropped things. The diagnosis was Parkinson's Disease, but I continued to work as long as I could. When I began messing up the diplomas I handwrote for the students, I decided it was time to find a new type of work. I talked with another missionary who also had an Associate School and he was willing to take my students so that they could continue their studies. This assured me that the Lord was closing the school for me and I boxed all my materials and shipped them to the missionary who would continue the work.

In 2010, Bob and I became members of a church near our home, McCalla Bible Church, pastored by Dr. John "Jay" Jackson. For several years, we served in children's ministry there and were blessed to be used by God to impart His truths to the young ones. Bob and I have had the privilege of seeing the majority of these children mature into godly young men and women who are serving in various ways which bless their families, their church and their communities. Some of these young people have gone on mission trips, and at least one of them is training to become a pastor. I can say that most were from Christian homes and had good guidance at home. We thank the Lord and give Him the credit for working in their young lives.

Things are beginning to change in our lives now. We are spending more time in doctors' offices and are dealing with issues that come with aging, but we still ask God to use our lives to assist and encourage the people He allows to enter our days. We thank the Lord for each new day He gives and pray that Bob's and my lives will continue to bring honor and glory to Him.

I have heard people say that missionaries sacrifice everything. That is very far from the truth in my experience! I do not feel that I sacrificed a thing. In fact, I gained so much from my experiences: such priceless gifts as the revelation of Himself, His power, His protection, His love, His mercy and His provision in every area of my life. How rich my life became through the addition of many brothers and sisters in the Lord! Sacrifice? No! Joy! The Lord gave me such a special privilege by calling me to serve Him. I thank you, Lord!

I have also heard people say that missionaries are people who do no wrong. They must have forgotten that Romans 3:23 says, "…all have sinned and fall short of the glory of God." There are no exceptions. We all fall short. We all need a Savior, and we all need the Holy Spirit in our daily walk. We are weak, but He is strong. He leads and I follow, knowing that when I fall, He will pick me up and guide me further in my walk.

I pray that the story of my life has been a blessing and inspiration to you. Under His watchful eye, may it be used as a tool to challenge readers to pray, to wait, to respond to His leading, to understand His unique call to each one. Just as I am sure that I was chosen before birth for the work God prepared for me, I am also sure that YOU were chosen before birth as well! May you grow in your knowledge of Him and in your understanding of the plan He has for you, a plan for you to honor Him in a way no one else can.

MY CHALLENGE

What are you thinking? The need is everywhere, throughout the world. Consider the areas of the Andes Mountains where people plead for missionaries to come and teach them about God. Consider areas where ethnic beliefs hold the people in darkness away from God's truth and where ancient practices lead to great evil. There are large gaps all over the world, places that have not been reached with the gospel of Jesus Christ. Will you allow God to place you in one of those gaps?

When God calls, He already has a place to which He will lead you. Do not try to take over. Your experiences will probably differ from those of other missionaries, so have no preconceived ideas about how things should be going. Consider, under God's leadership, where the need is greater and where God could use your service more. Is there a work for you where the gospel is already established? Make sure of His direction. Don't go in search of adventure even though adventure does sometimes come along with the job. Each person's call will be different, but the important thing is to be sure that it's God's call. People need the Lord, and each of us can do our part to meet that need in various ways.

Be patient. Do not go off half-cocked. Wait and pray. God has His timing for your life. My call to missions was very direct and clear. I was left with no doubt in my heart. I knew I had been called by God. The service and work resulted in joy in the Lord. There remains a hunger in my soul to continue the work of the Lord. Peace and assurance claimed my soul. Seek that assurance and confirmation in your own life.

Interact with missionaries. Familiarize yourself with a missionary who is serving in the type of work you feel the Lord is leading you to do. Learn from other missionaries about the needs. Take short mission trips. Keep an open mind about the work you will do.

Seek support- financial, emotional, spiritual, and physical- through a mission board or independently. It is my belief that it is better to go through a mission board because a board can provide encouragement and counsel when needed.

Pray. Pray about specific needs and concerns. Think seriously about the fact that people need the Lord everywhere. I suggest that great prayer and consideration be given to your choice of location. You might not know right away. The Lord may lead you to a mission board where there is a need in your particular area of interest or ability. People in the cities have many opportunities to hear the message via missionaries and television and radio, but there are many in remote parts of the world who have never heard and who have no way of hearing. Ask the Lord if He might lead you to take the good news to those who need to hear it. Let me say again, there is a great unmet need in many unreached areas of the world, areas where ethnic beliefs hold the people in darkness. Will you be the one to take the light of the gospel to them?

"And my God will supply all your needs according to His riches in glory in Christ Jesus." Philippians 4:19

"Pray without ceasing; in everything give thanks; for this is God's will for you in Christ Jesus." I Thessalonians 5:17-18

"But you, beloved, building yourselves up on your most holy faith, praying in the Holy Spirit, keep yourselves in the love of God, waiting anxiously for the mercy of our Lord Jesus Christ to eternal life" Jude 20-21.

Printed in the United States
By Bookmasters